AS-Level
Sociology

Dictionary
Key Terms and Concepts

Contents

Section One — The Dictionary Entries

Section Two — Key Terms and Questions

This book is suitable for both the AQA and OCR AS-level Specifications.

There are notes at the top of each of the lists of key terms and questions to tell you if there's a bit you can ignore for your syllabus.

Editors:
Chris Downham, Tim Major, Kate Redmond, Katherine Reed, Edward Robinson
Contributors:
Sarah Acford-Palmer, Linda Parkins, Carol Potter, Andy Walker
Proofreaders:
Sarah Acford-Palmer, Simon Little, Rachel Selway, Emma Singleton

Published by Coordination Group Publications Ltd.

ISBN: 1-84146-947-5
Groovy website: www.cgpbooks.co.uk
Jolly bits of clipart from CorelDRAW
Printed by Elanders Hindson, Newcastle upon Tyne.

absenteeism   Taking time off from work without good reason. If this is organised so as to deliberately decrease efficiency, it is considered to be a form of **industrial action**.

action theory   Type of sociological theory that suggests culture is determined by the behaviour and interaction of individuals. Compare to **structural theory**.

affluent workers   Workers who are paid well for doing boring jobs. **Goldthorpe et al.** found that these workers did not feel alienated as a result of having to do a dull job because the high pay allowed them to enjoy a good lifestyle outside of work.

agenda-setting   A practice in journalism where an editor or journalist selects what to include in the news and chooses a particular angle to take when reporting it, so affecting how the story is perceived by their audience.

agitator   A worker who encourages colleagues to feel dissatisfied with their working conditions. May help to provoke strikes or other **industrial action**.

alienation of labour   A situation where work has become a series of boring or meaningless tasks, and workers have no control over their activities. See **Blauner**.

allocation function   Sorting people into appropriate jobs depending on their skills.

Althusser   Neo-**Marxist** sociologist who saw education as part of the "ideological state apparatus". He argued that education is designed to produce a docile and obedient workforce.

anomie   **Durkheim**'s term for a state of moral confusion in society, resulting from an absence of the common shared norms and values that bind a society together. He argued that this was bad for both individuals (who are uncertain of how to behave in particular situations) and for society as a whole. Anomie (or "normlessness") is a state that is typical of societies undergoing sudden change.

Ansley (1972) **Marxist feminist** who argued that men who are frustrated by their low status and lack of control at work tend to take out this frustration on women, instead of challenging the capitalist system.

anti-school subculture   Group that rejects school rules and refuses to conform in school. They are often formed by working-class pupils. See **Willis**.

Aries (1962) Described a "cult of the child" in modern Western European culture. He argued that, before **industrialisation**, children took on adult work as soon as they were physically able and weren't treated much differently from adults. He used medieval paintings as evidence of this. He argued that it was during industrialisation that the belief that children needed specialised care and nurturing had developed.

Atkinson (1986) British economist who claimed that **post-Fordist** companies organise their workers into **core workers**, who are mostly white and male, and **peripheral workers**, who are disproportionately black and female.

automation   A situation where technology becomes used in work previously done by employees. It often involves job losses and **deskilling**. **Zuboff** described its possible effects on the workplace.

Bagdikian (1997) **Marxist** writer who demonstrated the increased monopolisation of American media. According to Bagdikian, in the 1980s the US media was controlled by 50 companies, but this had declined to just 10 companies by 1997.

Ballard (1994) In a study of Punjabi Sikhs in Leeds, Ballard discovered that ethnic identity was passed from one generation to the next. However, children developed multiple presentations of themselves, e.g. they kept an attachment to their parents' culture while acting in more westernised ways outside the home.

Bandura, Ross and Ross (1963) Conducted psychological experiments that demonstrated how boys imitated aggression in films they had watched. Their research has been used to support the **hypodermic syringe theory** of the media.

Barker (1984) Her study of the Moonies (Unification Church) demonstrates how **qualitative** research can help to explain statistical links. The study used **triangulation**: she carried out interviews, observations and questionnaires.

Baudrillard (1988) Influential in **Postmodernism**, Baudrillard said that society has become media-saturated, i.e. full of different signs and images which can be interpreted in different ways. Baudrillard said that people merge what they see in the media with their own everyday experiences to make their own individual sense of reality — see **hyperreality**.

Becker (1971) Conducted research based on interviews with 60 teachers from Chicago High Schools. Becker argued that teachers tended to share an image of the "ideal pupil", which was closely related to middle class pupils in terms of appearance, personality and speech.

bedroom subculture An argument put forward by **McRobbie and Garber** (1976). They believed that girls accept social control but gain private space by spending a lot of time in their bedrooms with friends discussing boyfriends and make-up and listening to music.

benefits Financial support paid by the **Welfare State** to individuals.
- **selective benefits** These are means-tested, i.e. they're paid to those most in need — e.g. housing benefit, jobseeker's allowance.
- **universal benefits** These are available to everyone in a designated position, e.g. all parents are entitled to child benefit.

Bennett (1999) Carried out research in Newcastle clubs and concluded that young people today form brief, temporary associations rather than subcultures because youth identity is now very fluid. Bennett called these associations **neo-tribes**; they are loose groups based around mix-and-match fashions and lifestyles.

Bernstein (1970) Identified two key speech patterns which were believed to have an effect on educational attainment:
- **Elaborated Code** Speech pattern characterised by clarity and precision so that ideas can be explicitly communicated between people who do not know each other. It often uses images to explain things in detail, and it is the language code predominantly used by teachers in schools.
- **Restricted Code** Speech pattern characterised by abbreviated phrases and used by people who are from the same social grouping, often used by the working class. It usually applies only to the situation the participants are in, as meanings are implicit, and Bernstein argued it was less able to articulate complex ideas.

Beveridge Report Report setting out the principles which informed the creation of the British **Welfare State** immediately after the Second World War. It was written by William Beveridge and its aim was to eliminate the "five great evils" of idleness, disease, ignorance, squalor and want. The Report proposed the introduction of social insurance to provide a universal, comprehensive and free NHS.

bias When information or material reflects a particular viewpoint, to the exclusion of others. It may give a false impression of a situation.

Biggs (1993) Conducted research which found that TV sitcoms tended to present negative stereotypes of the elderly, whilst soap operas were dominated by middle aged or older people.

biomedical model of health This is the conventional Western view of health. It sees the body as a biological machine with each part of the body performing a function. The doctors' job is to restore these functions by curing the problem. See **Hart**. Compare with the **social model of health**.

Blauner (1964) A **technological determinist** who believed increased technology in the workplace led to a lack of power and satisfaction for workers, leading to a sense of **alienation**. Blauner discovered that workers suffered varying levels of alienation depending on the type of industry they worked in.

Blumler and Katz (1974) Argued that the audience uses the media to meet their needs. They developed the **uses and gratifications theory**, in which everyone chooses the media that suits their needs.

Bott (1957) Studied **conjugal roles** of married couples and identified two main ways household jobs can be shared:

- **joint roles** Husbands and wives have flexible tasks and responsibilities are shared. Leisure is also shared as there are loose social networks with wider family.
- **segregated roles** Husbands and wives have distinct traditional responsibilities within the family. Wives keep close social networks with wider female kin.

Boulton (1983) Carried out a study of **conjugal roles** in dual career families. Boulton found that, even though men helped out with specific elements of childcare such as bath-time, the overall responsibility was still primarily with women.

Bourdieu French **Marxist** who argued that the upper class maintains its position at the top of society by upper class parents passing on **cultural capital** to their children. He said that the middle class try to develop cultural capital in their children, putting them at an advantage in education, but that working class children don't develop it.

bourgeoisie **Marxist** term for the class who owns the means of production: the bourgeoisie own the land, machinery, factories etc., and have the power to "hire and fire" workers. Marx believed the bourgeoisie made very large profits at the expense of the workers' health and well-being. The bourgeoisie have control of the **superstructure** and so create an **ideology** which supports their position.

Bowles and Gintis (1976) **Marxist** sociologists who argued that there was a close connection between relations in the workplace and in education; a "correspondence principle". They said that the workplace requires a hard-working, passive and obedient workforce and the education system helps to produce this type of workforce via the **hidden curriculum**. Hmm, I wonder how many teachers would describe their classes as hard-working, passive and obedient..?

Braverman (1974) Said that work is degraded by industrial capitalism. The Braverman Thesis, or "Deskilling Thesis", said that **mechanisation** leaves workers with low-paid and unfulfilling work, because work becomes **deskilled**. He said this situation would get worse as technology developed.

British Attitudes Survey (1991) A large scale study of 1000 married couples which found that, although there was more sharing of child-rearing tasks than in the past, there was less  equality with household tasks. The survey concluded that there was some movement towards a more equal division of labour but that this was a slow process.

British Sociological Association The professional association for sociologists in the UK. The BSA has issued ethical guidelines for sociologists to follow when carrying out their research.

Bruce (1995) Sociologist who looked at the role of religion in society. Bruce said that many of **Troeltsch**'s findings don't apply any more because of **religious pluralism** in modern society. Bruce studied **New Age movements**, identifying three themes:

- **New Ecology** Movements that are based around concern for the environment.
- **New Psychology** Movements that see the self as sacred.
- **New Science** Movements that reject the claims of traditional science.

Busfield (2001) Feminist who said that women are more likely than men to be diagnosed as **mentally ill**. She said that this is because doctors, the majority of whom are male, interpret women's behaviour more negatively.

Butler Act This was the 1944 Education Act. The act's declared aims were to provide equality of educational opportunity, free education for all, and three distinct periods of schooling for children: primary, secondary and the option at 15 to attend further and higher education. The act is most famous for introducing the tripartite system of secondary education — three different types of secondary school which were designed to meet the needs of pupils according to their age, aptitude and ability:

- **grammar schools** For the 20% of pupils who passed their 11+ exam. They were taught traditional subjects ready for university.
- **secondary modern schools** Offered basic education for the 75-80% of children who failed the 11+ exam.
- **technical schools** Provided vocational education for 5% of pupils, although these were only available in certain parts of the country.

Calvinism A strict form of Protestant Christianity which emerged in the 17th century. Calvinists believed in predestination — that whether they were destined to go to heaven or hell was already decided by God. However, they also believed that hard work and a moral life were signs that God favoured them. These Calvinist beliefs encouraged people to work hard. Max **Weber** suggested that Calvinism and the resulting "protestant work ethic" were important in the development of industrial **capitalism**.

Campbell (1981, 1986) She studied female crime, including women in New York gangs. She found that official statistics often underestimated female crime rates. She also found that female suspects were more likely than male suspects to be cautioned rather than prosecuted.

Cantril (1940) Studied the audience response to the famous *War of the Worlds* broadcast in 1938. This radio broadcast was an adaptation of an HG Wells story and included fake news bulletins about Martians invading Earth. Some radio listeners believed the fake bulletins were true and panicked (silly people). Cantril studied this from the viewpoint of **cultural effects theory**, saying that the audience's response was caused by the cultural context in which it was heard. At the time of the broadcast, there was insecurity in American society as a result of economic depression and the threat of war in Europe. People wouldn't have been surprised to hear really bad news on the radio, and this meant they were more likely to believe the fake news bulletins.

capitalism An economic system based on private ownership of the means of production, distribution and exchange of **commodities**. In the capitalist system, labour itself becomes a commodity. Employers buy workers' labour in return for wages, and sell what the workers make for profit. Capitalism is associated with free trade and individual enterprise. It is the dominant economic philosophy in Western countries. Compare with **Marxism** and **socialism**.

care in the community A social policy, introduced in the 1980s, where people with mental health problems are looked after in the community, instead of in institutions. Care in the community was a response to concerns over the **institutionalisation** of mentally ill people, as voiced by **Goffman**. It can create a positive environment for people with mental health problems to live. In some cases though, it has been criticised for leading to patient neglect and harm to both patients and the community.

Cartwright and O'Brien (1976) They found that middle class patients had a better relationship with their doctors than working class patients. For example, working class patients had shorter consultations with their doctors than middle class patients — working class patients therefore received a lower level of care. They concluded that the main reason for this was the readiness and ability of middle class patients to ask questions.

case study   An in-depth study of a particular event, individual or group. Often a case study is chosen because it is believed to be representative of a wider group or trend.

catharsis theory   This theory suggests that seeing violence on TV helps viewers release tension and violent thoughts, making them less likely to commit violent acts themselves.

censorship   The control of the media (TV, newspapers, film etc.) through banning certain scenes, images or language from being broadcast or published.

census   A government survey of all people within a defined geographical area. The British census is an obligatory survey of the entire population every ten years. It's an important source of secondary data on the changing characteristics (housing, education, work patterns etc.) of the British population.

childhood   The period when someone is considered to be a child. Childhood is a **social construct** — ideas about when childhood ends and adulthood begins vary over time and between different cultures. The term "childhood" is often used to refer to the first stage in someone's life when they are dependent on other people (especially their parents).

church   A well-established religious organisation. Churches are hierarchical and often have a bureaucratic structure. They are integrated into mainstream society, and often have a close relationship with the state. Examples include the Roman Catholic Church, and the Church of England.

civil religion   This is a **Functionalist** idea, which suggests that secular (non-religious) symbols and rituals are used to bind society together and create social cohesion. Civil religion reinforces the loyalty and respect that individuals have for society. E.g. in the USA, aspects of civil religion include Thanksgiving Day, Veterans' Day and saluting the flag.

Clarke and Critcher (1985) Neo-**Marxist** sociologists who claimed that the state and the leisure industry have contributed to **leisure** becoming commercialised. They argue that leisure now involves the passive consumption of "leisure commodities" (e.g. holidays, games, TV). In their view, the state limits leisure opportunities and promotes bourgeois values through licensing and censorship, while the leisure industry manipulates people's choices and tastes in order to make profit.

class   A way of stratifying society, on the basis of people's social and economic status. Class is hierarchical — some classes are more privileged than others. The "class system" was heavily criticised by **Marxists**.

closed question   A question which requires a "yes" or "no" answer, or has multiple choice options to choose from. Closed questions tend to generate reliable **quantitative data** (and tend to be quite popular with people who haven't done enough revision for their exams).

Coates and Silburn (1970)   They studied poverty in Nottingham. They concluded that there are **situational constraints** which prevent people from breaking out of poverty. Examples of situational constraints include: lack of educational and employment opportunities, poor housing conditions and a higher incidence of long-term illness. Coates and Silburn suggested that the behaviour of people living in poverty is a reaction to their disadvantaged social situation rather than being the product of an alternative culture. Their views are a response to **cultural deprivation theories** of poverty.

coercive pacification   See **Pollert**.

Cohen, Albert (1955) **Functionalist** sociologist who said that working class boys form **subcultures** because they can have high status in them, even though they might feel like failures at school. The formation of subcultures is a reaction to "status frustration" (having low status). In "delinquent subcultures", individuals reject middle class values and can achieve status and approval within the group by performing **deviant** acts like vandalism.

Cohen, Phil (1972) Studied East End youth culture. He argued that the break-up of family and communal life had created a "cultural vacuum" in the lives of young working class men. He suggested that the emerging youth cultures represented an attempt to deal with this "loss" by forming a type of community. Cohen said that "Mod" subcultures were an attempt to copy the lifestyles of East Enders who had "escaped" into better paid jobs, while "Skinhead" subcultures were an exaggerated form of working class lifestyle.

Cohen, Stan (1973) Examined the way the media reported spectacular **subcultures** in the 1960s, e.g. the Mods and Rockers. He said the media often represented these subcultures in a negative and exaggerated way, which could result in a "**moral panic**" among the general public.

Cohen and Young (1981) Authors of *The Manufacture of News*, which described how the news is influenced by practical constraints. They argued that the news is not always as factual and objective as it purports to be, because of time, technical and budget constraints.

Colley (1998) Studied secondary **socialisation** in schools. She found that some subjects are seen as more masculine or feminine than others.

commodities   Materials, services or labour which have a monetary value.

comparative method   Comparing societies which are culturally or historically different using **secondary data**. An example is **Durkheim**'s 1897 study of suicide.

comprehensive schools   In 1965, the Labour Government reorganised the state secondary school system to try and make it more equal. The old **tripartite system** was abolished. All pupils in the state educational system now went to comprehensive schools, and they didn't have to take an 11+ exam.

conformity   Adherence to the norms and values of society. The opposite of **deviance**.

conjugal roles   The roles of husband and wife (or partners) within the home. See **Bott** and **Edgell**.

consensus   Fundamental agreement within a society about that society's basic values. **Functionalist** theory suggests that, as a result of **socialisation**, the people in a society all share the same norms and values and this contributes to consensus.

constraint   An external restraining social influence on an individual's behaviour, leading them to conform to society's norms and values, e.g. laws.

control group   A group of people in an experiment who are not exposed to the experimental stimulus under study. The groups who have been exposed to the stimulus can then be compared to the control group.

core worker   A feature of **post-Fordism** identified by John **Atkinson**. Core workers are permanent, full-time, multi-skilled and highly motivated employees (and tend to be mostly white and male).

correlation The association between two **variables** where changes in one variable result in changes in the other variable, but do not necessarily cause them. E.g. Government statistics show a correlation between achievement in schools and social **class**, but there may be other factors affecting achievement.

credibility The integrity or "believability" of **secondary data**.

crime A violation of criminal law.

critical junctures A concept introduced by Jon Clark. The moment at which, during the introduction of a new technology to a workplace, workers can influence the way in which that technology is used. Once this moment has passed, it becomes difficult for workers to change their relationship to the new technology.

cross media ownership When one company owns different forms of media, e.g. Rupert Murdoch's News Corporation owns TV stations and newspapers.

Croteau and Hoynes (2000) Studied media **stereotypes** of women. They found that a major cause of stereotyped media messages about women was that newspaper and TV management was male dominated, e.g. only 6% of top American newspaper management in the 1990s was female.

cult An often transient and informal religious group whose members are generally recruited from young or disadvantaged people in a state of emotional crisis. Cults are loosely organised and often governed by charismatic leadership.

cultural capital Wealth that is in the form of ideas and values, e.g. the language and culture of the dominant class. Working class children are said to be hindered in education by a lack of cultural capital; similarly working class adults are said to be less likely to achieve high status employment. See **Bourdieu**.

cultural deprivation theory The theory that educational achievement and health vary according to social class because some classes lack the cultural values and knowledge which promote a healthy lifestyle and educational achievement.

cultural effects theory The theory that different people interpret the media in different ways, according to their social context. See **Cantril**.

culture The "way of life" of a society or group. Culture is made up of things such as language, customs, knowledge, norms and values and is passed on by socialisation. Culture varies between societies and within societies over time. See also **subculture**.

culture of dependency A **New Right** theory which asserts that welfare benefits are too high, discouraging people from working and encouraging the development of an **underclass** which develops a subculture that is resistant to work. See **Murray**.

Cumberbatch (1990) Studied gender issues in the media. He found women were under-represented and often **stereotyped** in advertising. When they did appear they were likely to be portrayed as young and attractive and situated in a non-work environment.

Cumberbatch and Negrine (1992) Found that disabled people are under-represented in the media. They said that the disabled only appeared in roles particularly about disability, often focussing on pity or comedy.

Daly (1973) Radical **feminist** who claimed that Christianity passes on male-dominated ideology through religious images, teachings and the **patriarchal** church **hierarchy**. Daly also suggested that Christianity itself is a patriarchal myth based on hatred of women.

Davis and Moore (1945) **Functionalists** who believed that modern society rewards ability, effort and intelligence. They claimed that there has to be a system of unequal rewards to motivate people to train for demanding and difficult jobs. The function of the education system is therefore to allocate people to appropriate occupations.

Dean and Taylor-Gooby (1992) **Weberians** who argue that changes in the UK labour market, such as less job security, have led to increased **poverty**. With part-time, short-term and casual work now common, people are more likely to experience poverty at some time in their lives.

deferred gratification Putting off immediate gratification in order to achieve a long-term goal. For example, this might involve studying and training for a well-paid professional career (and putting off the immediate gratification of earning a full wage at sixteen). See **Sugarman**, who claimed that working class culture lacked a belief in the importance of deferred gratification.

Delphy and Leonard (1992) Radical **feminists** who see the family as a **patriarchal** institution in which women do most of the work and men get most of the benefit.

denomination A well-established subset of a religion, e.g. Methodism is a denomination of Christianity.

desacrilisation The process by which religious and spiritual beliefs come to have less influence in society.

design for life A culture of social apathy and resignation to **poverty** identified by **Lewis** in poor communities. Lewis claimed that this culture is initially a response to poverty, but that it is then passed via **socialisation** to future generations and so becomes a cause of future poverty.

deskilling When work comes to involve less expertise, flexibility and skill as a result of **mechanisation** — see **Braverman**.

deviance Any behaviour that is different to what is regarded as "normal" or socially acceptable, e.g. girls being loud and violent. The opposite of **conformity**.

differentiation The process by which different areas of society become more specialised. This means that some institutions in society have fewer functions and a narrower circle of influence than they did before. For example, the Church has less influence over education and politics than it once did, because new specialised institutions have evolved to control these things since the 19th century.

discourse Any kind of discussion or communication (either written or spoken) about a subject.

disengagement The increasing separation of the Church from the state, and the decline of its influence on society as a whole.

Dobash and Dobash (1979, 1992) Radical **feminists** who argued that men use violence against women as a form of power and control. They claim that there is still cultural support for a man's "right" to discipline his wife in Britain's **patriarchal** society.

Douglas (1964) Studied the link between **class** and educational achievement. Douglas suggested that both cultural and material deprivation play a part in underachievement at school by working class children. He identified a link between poor living conditions and underachievement, but also claimed that working class parents seemed less interested in the education of their children than middle class parents did.

Doyal and Pennell (1979) **Marxist** sociologists who claimed that the pursuit of profit in **capitalist** society has negative health consequences for working class people. Working class jobs can be physically and psychologically dangerous — industrial injuries and disease are common. Overtime and shift work can be damaging to health, and the drive towards bigger profits keeps wages low, leading to **poverty** and all the health risks associated with it.

Driver and Ballard (1981) Studied the link between **ethnicity** and education. They found that high parental expectations in Asian families increase educational achievement.

Durkheim (b. 1858 d. 1917) The founder of **Functionalism**. He was one of the three most influential figures in shaping the modern discipline of Sociology, together with **Weber** and **Marx**. Durkheim introduced many important sociological concepts, including the "collective consciousness of society" (the shared **norms** and **values** that bind a society together) and "**anomie**" (a state of being without these norms). Durkheim also wrote extensively on the subject of suicide and on the sociology of **religion**.

Dutton (1986) Studied how news is selected and presented by the media, especially the practice of **gate-keeping** in journalism. The "gate" is opened for some news stories but closed for others. He found that news editors filter potential news material out because there's usually too much for the amount of space available.

ecclesia **Weber**'s term for an official national religion — a universal and all-encompassing church such as the Church of England.

Edgell (1980) Studied **conjugal roles** and division of labour in a sample of 38 middle-class couples to test out **Willmott and Young**'s theory that families were now more balanced with the sharing of domestic duties. Edgell found that housework was still not shared equally, but there was increased sharing of childcare between men and women. He found that half of husbands and two thirds of wives thought that sexual equality in decision-making was a bad thing.

Edwards and Scullion (1982) **Marxist** sociologists who compared seven factories in Britain to study conflict and consent at work. They said that differences of interest between managers and workers mean that there is always potential for conflict, including **strikes**. They concluded that particular management strategies produce particular types of conflict.

Eisenstadt (1956, 1967) From a **Functionalist** perspective, Eisenstadt said that **subcultures** form because people in today's society feel that they need to achieve their status. Eisenstadt said that society segregates young people and allocates them to a marginal, transitional status that leads to insecurity and identity problems. Youth subcultures give them security within a community and a clear **status**.

Engels (1884) A sociologist, philosopher and co-founder of **Marxism**, Engels was a German factory owner but nevertheless a fierce critic of **capitalism**. He said women were subordinated through institutions of private property and monogamy. Engels argued that the family had the economic function of keeping wealth within the **bourgeoisie** because parents pass it on to the next generation as inheritance.

ethics A set of principles about what's morally right and wrong. Ethics of sociological research say you should use informed consent if at all possible — i.e. the people taking part in the research should know about it and agree to it — unless it is absolutely necessary to deceive the participants, in which case they should be told immediately afterwards. So that's alright then. Sort of.

ethnicity The cultural background a group of people share, not necessarily the same as nationality. Ethnicity is a shared cultural **identity**, which may include **values**, **norms** of behaviour, language and **religion**.

ethnography Research which studies the culture and way of life of a community. It is usually done by participant or non-participant **observation**, and may also use **interviews** and **case studies**. Ethnography looks at social relationships, organisations, customs and practices. It is an interactionist approach to sociological study and so produces **qualitative data**.

Eversley and Bonnerjea (1982) Studied how family structure is related to **class**. They found that middle class areas in the UK have a higher proportion of **nuclear families**, and that inner-city working class areas have a higher proportion of lone-parent households. Eversley and Bonnerjea also found that there is a relationship between locality and family type, e.g. the coastal areas of England and Wales contain an increasing proportion of elderly one or two person households, and these people may be isolated from close relations.

extended family   A family made up of parents, offspring and other relatives. Families can be either vertically extended with three or more generations living together or horizontally extended in the same generation, e.g. with two or more brothers living together with their respective wives and children. Sociologically, the term "modified extended family" can also refer to relatives who live in close proximity with regular interactions, obligations and responsibilities, even though they may not live in the same house.

Eysenck (1971)   Argued that the genetic component of intelligence is the most important factor affecting educational achievement. He said, controversially, that differences in achievement were connected to the relative intelligence levels of different socio-economic and ethnic groups.

false consciousness   An inaccurate way of seeing the world. It's a **Marxist** theory that says the working class has absorbed and become committed to values and beliefs that serve and support the interests of the ruling **capitalist** class. This false consciousness is passed on by ideological control, e.g. through education, media and religion. Marxist theory says that this stops the **proletariat** from uniting and overthrowing the ruling class.

false needs   Things people think they need but which don't really satisfy them, e.g. the "need" to own an iPod, a new kitchen or a flash car. According to **Marxists**, these false needs have been created by a capitalist culture which encourages consumerism. The **mass media** plays a significant role in persuading people that they "need" these goods. E.g. you watch a James Bond film and see expensive hotels, watches, cars and clothes — it encourages you to desire those things. See **Marcuse**.

family   A type of household consisting of people who are usually but not always related by **kinship**. The family is the agent of primary **socialisation** for most people. Family forms vary across cultures and even within cultures.

family structure   The way families are made up. **Functionalists** suggest that this changed as a result of **industrialisation**: in pre-industrial society, **extended families** were most common and in industrial society the **nuclear family** became dominant. However, many sociologists disagree with this view.

Featherstone and Hepworth (1995)   Studied the magazine *Retirement Choice* in order to analyse media messages about age. They found that an image of "youthful" old people was used in order to appeal to the expanding market of older people with active consumer lifestyles.

femininity   Appearance and behaviour that is considered most appropriate for girls and women. Although it is often seen as "natural", ideas about what is feminine are socially constructed through **socialisation** and vary between different societies, cultures and historical periods. Even within a society, there are likely to be several different ideas about femininity, for example ideas may vary between social classes, age groups and ethnicities. See **Ferguson**, **McRobbie**.

feminisation of masculinity   The idea that images and perceptions of masculinity are becoming more feminine. This is part of changing social constructions of **gender**. **Rutherford** used the sale and marketing of men's cosmetic products and toiletries as evidence for this process. There are now far more of these products than there were in the past, and images used to advertise them are often of half-naked male models. This is similar to the way cosmetics are marketed at women.

feminism   A movement which believes that social organisations and culture have been dominated by men to the exclusion of women. Feminists claim this has devalued and disadvantaged women into a marginalized status. And they're not too pleased about it.

- **black feminism**   Focuses on the fact that ethnic background also affects women's life experiences.
- **liberal feminism**   Believes that **socialisation** reproduces gender divisions and that social change is possible by putting pressure on the legal system and government to change laws that discriminate against women.
- **Marxist feminism**   Says that **capitalism** is responsible for the exploitation of women, e.g. because housework and childcare are unpaid. This provides the next generation of workers free of charge to the state. It also makes workers who have dependants less likely to take **industrial action**.
- **radical feminism**   Believes that men have always exploited women, as opposed to society being responsible. Radical feminists believe that changing the law is not enough on its own — ideas also have to be changed, e.g. by positive discrimination.

Ferguson   (1983) Used content analysis and **interviews** to research three of the best-selling women's magazines. She argued that they instructed women in the values and attitudes of being a woman. She coined the phrase "cult of **femininity**" to describe the way in which these magazines reinforced **stereotypes** of women as sexual, domestic and romantic.

Ferri and Smith   (1996) Studied **conjugal roles**. Found that two thirds of full-time working mothers said they were responsible for cooking and cleaning, and four fifths said they were responsible for laundry. In their research in 1998, Ferri and Smith found little evidence that full-time employment of both parents leads to the erosion of family life.

field experiment   A type of experiment that takes place in a real social setting, but which is still controlled by the researcher in order to answer a sociological question. Used by **interactionist** sociologists. Compare with **lab experiment**, **natural experiment**.

Fiske   (1988) Said that individuals become very experienced readers of the media. He argued that people can understand one **media text** in different ways on different levels, and in relation to other media texts on the same subject. See **selective filter model**.

flexible worker   A worker who can carry out different but related tasks. In the post-**Fordist** era, flexible specialisation has become more common. As companies become more flexible, they need more flexible workers.

folk devil   A group or individual popularly represented as evil and a threat to society, used as a scapegoat for society's problems. Stan **Cohen** used this term to describe the way "Mods and Rockers" were presented in the media in the 1960s.

Fordism   A type of industrial production based on **scientific management**, first used by car manufacturer Henry Ford. It uses a moving assembly line, with workers performing small, Henry Ford specialised tasks. This produces standardised parts for mass-produced products.

- **post-Fordism**   Theory that work now tends to be more flexible and less repetitive than it was at the height of **Fordism**. Post-Fordism involves computer technology, multi-skilled workers, a less strict hierarchy, new organisation of workers (see **Atkinson**) and products made for quality rather than quantity.
- **neo-Fordism**   A response to the **post Fordist** idea that computer technology is reducing the **deskilling** and **alienation of labour** that characterised **Fordism**. Neo-Fordists argue that in fact not much has changed for the working class, and that

there are just new methods of control. See **Thompson**, **Pollert**.

Friedmann (1977) Studied the impact of technology on the workplace. He disagreed with the **Braverman** thesis — Friedmann believed that workers can influence the application of technology, arguing that they can use their power of resistance. He said that market forces also have an impact on how technology is used.

Fuller (1980) Studied how **ethnicity** affects educational achievement. Found that Afro-Caribbean girls in London, who resented negative **stereotypes** both of being black and of being female, formed a **subculture** that resisted negative labelling and worked hard to gain success.

Functionalism An important sociological perspective about how society works, founded by **Durkheim.** Functionalists believe that society is made up of a number of institutions, each of which has a useful function and helps society to run smoothly, e.g. the family, the education system, religion. These institutions work in harmony because they have agreed **norms** and **values**, and this is essential for society to survive. Functionalists say that individuals internalise these norms and values (**socialisation**).

fundamentalism A movement in any **religion** which is committed to a literal, fundamental interpretation of religious texts. The supporters of these movements want to return to what they see as the true basis of the religion.

Gans (1974) Described how journalists choose to select and present the news, including the journalistic practice of **gate-keeping**.

gate-keeping A practice in journalism through which news items are either chosen or rejected for broadcast or publication. The "gate" is opened for some news items but closed for others. It's affected by the editor/journalist's **news values**, and is important in understanding how the news is socially constructed.

gender The social (as opposed to biological) characteristics used to categorise people as either male or female.

- **gender roles** The social expectations of masculine and feminine behaviour, including speech, dress, opinions, etc. Gender roles are a **social construct** and therefore change over time, e.g. in the past women in the UK were mostly seen as having domestic responsibilities, but are now often likely to be interested in a career.

- **gender socialisation** The process through which boys and girls are taught to behave in a way that is "normal" for their gender, e.g. girls are often encouraged to behave in a way that is "ladylike". See **Oakley**.

Gershuny (1992) Studied changes in attitudes towards **masculinity**. He found that childcare and housework are more equally shared between men and women in modern relationships than they were in the past. Gershuny also identified an increase in the number of househusbands — men who stay at home to do housework while their female partners go out to work.

Gillborn (1990) **Interactionist** sociologist who studied **ethnicity** in education. Gillborn suggested that teachers negatively label black children, and referred to the "myth of the black challenge", i.e. teachers seeing Afro-Caribbean students as a challenge to authority. This process could be a cause of the high exclusion rates seen amongst black pupils — see **self-fulfilling prophecy**.

Gillespie (1995) Studied the construction of new "hybrid" ethnic identities. Gillespie's study focused on how young Sikhs mixed together mainstream western culture with Punjabi traditions.

Gilroy (1982) Studied the social reasons for black crime. He argued that crime was a rational political response to racial discrimination, and reflected young black people's anger at prejudice in white society. Gilroy also suggested that black criminality is exaggerated by an **institutionally racist** police force and mass media.

Gittins (1993) Studied the social reasons for the rising divorce rate. She concluded that women were less willing to accept unhappy relationships. She believed that this showed a significant change away from formerly passive female **gender** roles.

Glasgow University Media Group (1976) (1980) (1982) Studied **bias** in the media. They found that TV coverage of workplace **strikes** in the 1970s was biased in favour of management and against the strikers in terms of the perspective, the language and what was covered.

Glennon and Butsch (1982) Studied class **stereotypes** on American TV. They concluded that professionals were over-represented as the heads of "TV families", and that working class characters tended to be shown as incompetent figures of fun.

globalisation The process of the world becoming more interconnected, leading to social and economic change. Globalisation is characterised by the breakdown of traditional national boundaries. It is caused by factors such as improved communications and technology, the growth of multinational companies and increased migration.

Goffman (1961) **Interactionist** who studied the behaviour of patients and staff in mental institutions. Goffman looked at how psychiatric patients become **institutionalised** in response to being negatively labelled as "mentally ill". Goffman developed the concept of **mortification of the self**.

Goldthorpe et al. (1969) **Weberians** who studied the attitudes of manual and white-collar workers to their jobs. They found that many **affluent workers** choose alienating work because of the external rewards (i.e. good pay) and did not expect job satisfaction.

Gough (1979) **Marxist** sociologist who considered the NHS to be a positive achievement gained by the working class through political action. Compare with **Navarro**.

Goulooze Dutch defensive midfielder who played for Derby County in the mid-1990s. Bald.

Gray (1992) Found that TV viewing patterns were related both to gender and to class. Working class women watched a lot more TV and videos than women in higher social classes did. They tended to use TV to shape their days of chores and childcare, while middle class women had a preference for "classic" and "quality" programmes, and treated viewing more as a **leisure** activity.

Greenberg et al. (1983) Studied American TV and found evidence of the over-representation of white people as characters in TV programmes. They found that 97% of characters on daytime soaps and dramas were white, and 87% of characters on primetime soaps and dramas were white.

Grint (1991) Sociologist who studied attitudes to work in past societies. Grint found that in classical societies like Ancient Greece, work was often looked down upon or not valued. Before the industrial revolution in the UK, work was seen as a necessary evil — Grint concluded that work has only been seen as important since **industrialisation**.

Grint and Woolgar (1992) Studied the way people talked about technology. They said that this **discourse** is crucial in determining how technology is applied. (This is the same **Grint** as the one above who studied people's attitudes to work — he's found a friend.)

Halevy (1927) **Marxist** who believed that **religion** is a conservative force, claiming that Methodism prevented **revolution** in the 19th century as it distracted the working class from their grievances. Halevy therefore saw religion as an inhibitor of major social change.

Hall (1982, 1992, 1996) New left sociologist who suggested that the media reinforces class identities by portraying the middle class positively and the working class negatively. Hall also identified how national and ethnic identities are **socialised** and how they can change over time.

Halsey (1980) Important writer on the sociology of education. Halsey studied the link between **material deprivation** and educational achievement. He claimed that the main factor preventing working class students staying on at school was lack of financial support.

happy robots A phrase used by **Marcuse** to describe workers who pursue media-induced "**false needs**" in their leisure time.

Hargreaves (1967) Sociologist who studied the creation of **deviant** pupil **subcultures** in schools. He claimed that working class pupils are often labelled as failures, which is why they reject the school's values in favour of delinquent values. Pupils are then able to award each other the status denied to them by school culture within their deviant group.

Hart (1985) Identified five features of the **biomedical model of health**:
1) Disease is physical.
2) Doctors are an elite.
3) Medicine is curative.
4) Illness is temporary.
5) Treatment is special.

Hartmann and Husband (1974) Analysed children's responses to ethnic minority stereotypes in the media. They found that children from areas with a low ethnic mix tended to accept negative media **stereotypes** about ethnic minorities, whereas children from areas with a high ethnic mix tended to reject the stereotypes.

Hawthorne Effect When people know they are part of an experiment, it affects their behaviour. This is called the Hawthorne Effect. This term derives from the Hawthorne investigations at the Western Electricity Company in Chicago by Elton Mayo. Variables such as temperature, lighting and break length were all changed to monitor the effect on worker productivity. However, it was found that it didn't matter whether the conditions were made better or worse — productivity usually increased when workers knew they were under observation.

Hebdige (1979) Studied "Punk" as a **subculture**. He suggested that "Punk" was a form of resistance to the dominant cultural values of 1970s Britain, and its symbolism stood for a rejection of common **norms** and **values** and a refusal to conform to them.

Heelas (1996) **Postmodernist** sociologist who studied the development of **New Age movements**. Found that they promote "self-spirituality" and development of the self. They therefore oppose the rejection of spirituality that has occurred in some modern societies, while avoiding a return to traditional religions. Compare with **secularisation**.

hegemony The dominance of a particular set of values in society. Law, religion, media, art, science, cinema and literature may be used to celebrate and make legitimate this one set of values and to discredit the alternatives. Important to neo-**Marxist** ideas about how the hegemonic values of the ruling class are spread by the **mass media**. Also used by neo-Marxists to explain why a revolutionary working class has not developed in modern capitalist economies.

Heidensohn (1986) **Feminist** sociologist who identified **gender** socialisation as an explanation of why females are involved in fewer crimes than males. Women are socialised into being emotional and domestic, which is less likely to lead to crime than qualities that men are socialised into, such as toughness and strength. Heidensohn also criticised sociologists for largely ignoring the 20% of all crimes that are committed by women.

Herberg (1956) American sociologist who added weight to the **secularisation** argument by claiming that church attendance shows commitment to the community, rather than to religion.

Hermes (1995) **Postmodernist** who said that people are able to respond to media **stereotypes** of women in a variety of ways. Hermes said that people are capable of rejecting **media messages** that conflict with their existing knowledge and experiences.

hidden curriculum (As opposed to the formal curriculum.) Involves the transmission of socially acceptable **norms**, **values** and attitudes to pupils during their time at school, e.g. punctuality, respect for authority, obedience. The hidden curriculum promotes social control. See **Bowles and Gintis**.

hierarchy A system in an organisation or in society that arranges people into an order of power and importance, with the highest ranked at the top and the lowest ranked at the bottom.

Hirschi (1969) Conservative criminologist who rejected ideas about the social causes of crime, saying that crime is a choice and down to individual responsibility. Hirschi argued that human beings are rational and will turn to crime when the advantages of crime appear to outweigh the disadvantages.

Hobson (1990) Studied how people in an office interpreted media messages. Hobson found that a few key individuals (**opinion leaders**) influenced what other people watched on television and their reactions to the programmes.

household A group of people who live together. Distinct from **family**, as members of a household are not necessarily related to each other, e.g. students sharing a house.

Howlett and Ashley (1991) Studied **cultural deprivation theory** — specifically inequalities in health. They found that middle class people are better informed about health issues, and so tend to follow healthier lifestyles.

husband controlled pooling Form of financial management in a family, in which the money is shared but the male partner makes most of the decisions about how to spend it. See **Pahl**.

Hyman (1967) American sociologist who argued that the "value system" of working class people creates a "self-imposed barrier to an improved position". So in Hyman's view, working class people tend not to value education and so they underachieve and are not able to improve their position.

hyperreality Concept introduced by the **postmodernist Baudrillard**. The situation where there are so many conflicting messages and images in everyday life that no single word or image has a straightforward meaning. Especially not words like "hyperreality".

hypodermic syringe theory The idea that the media injects its message directly into the minds of the audience. It claims that all people in the audience are affected in the same way, and that they're powerless to resist or reject the message.

hypothesis A proposition which is put forward for testing or appraisal. A hypothesis in sociology is usually a generalisation about a social phenomenon — e.g. "working class boys do badly at school because of material deprivation." Research could then be done to find out how correct this hypothesis is.

hypothetico-deductive model Research method favoured by **positivist** sociologists which mirrors the approach used in natural science. It involves using an experiment to test a **hypothesis** and then using the results to confirm, modify or reject the hypothesis.

iatrogenesis Illness that's caused by modern medicine. **Illich** says there are three types:

- **clinical iatrogenesis** Harm caused by poor treatments or diagnoses.
- **cultural iatrogenesis** The destruction of traditional ways of dealing with illness.
- **social iatrogenesis** Dependency on modern medicine, leading to the medical profession having considerable social control. Involves the medicalisation of natural areas of life, e.g. childbirth, ageing.

identity An individual's sense of self. This can be influenced by social factors such as **class**, **gender**, **religion** and **ethnicity**.

ideology A set of beliefs about the way things should be — often politically motivated.

Illich (1971, 1975) Radical sociologist, critical of modern medicine (see **iatrogenesis**) and education. He claimed that people in modern society had become dependent on professionals and experts for meeting these fundamental needs. He argued that traditional approaches are thus destroyed, and people become passive consumers of often harmful services. He said we should "deschool society", allowing people lifelong access to education according to their needs.

immediate gratification Enjoying pleasures now, rather than working towards future rewards. Highlighted by **Sugarman** as a feature of working class cultural attitudes towards education. Compare with **deferred gratification**.

industrial action When workers take action during conflict with their employers. Includes **strikes**, **work to rule**, sabotage or theft of company equipment and **absenteeism**.

industrialisation The extensive development of industry. Pre-industrial society tends to be largely agricultural and people's work centres on the home, farm, village and market. The process of industrialisation involves work becoming more mechanised, the creation of factories and the growth of cities.

industrialism Mechanised production by workers in industrial plants and factories. The production process is managed and coordinated by specialist managers. See **Fordism**, **Taylor**.

infrastructure In **Marxist** theory, the infrastructure is the economic base of society — the means of production and the relations of production. The infrastructure helps to shape the **superstructure** of society.

institutionalisation The process by which inmates or patients at "total institutions" like prisons or psychiatric hospitals become unable to manage on their own outside the institution. See **Goffman**.

institutional racism Policies, attitudes and culture of an organisation or society which, sometimes inadvertently, discriminate against ethnic minority groups.

Interactionism A school of sociological thought that says all individuals interpret society in their own way, and that human behaviour is not the product of external social laws. Society is seen as the product of interaction between individuals who have free will and free choice. Sometimes called Interpretivism. Compare with **positivism**.

internalisation The acceptance and adoption of social **norms** and **values** as a result of **socialisation**.

Interpretivism See **Interactionism**.

intertextual response **Postmodernist** concept — the process by which people can understand one **media text** in different ways and on different levels at the same time, e.g. watching a soap on TV because you're caught up in the drama and also because you like one of the actors. Emphasises the power of the individual to control his or her experience of the media. See **Fiske**.

interview Method of obtaining data by asking an interviewee a series of questions.

- **structured interviews** These ask the same **closed questions** for each interviewee, to get **quantitative data**.
- **unstructured interviews** These ask **open-ended questions**, which can vary for each interviewee, to get **qualitative data**.

interview effect When the response given by an interviewee isn't what they really think. This might be because they don't feel comfortable talking openly to the interviewer, or because they are influenced by the views and personality of the interviewer to respond a certain way. This "interview effect" means that data from interviews can sometimes be unreliable.

inverse care law The theory that the people with the greatest need for good healthcare are the least likely to get it. First suggested by **Tudor Hart**.

isolated mass theory **Kerr and Siegel**'s theory that workers who are geographically and socially isolated, e.g. dockers and miners, are more likely to strike because they have a strong sense of community and solidarity.

Jefferson (1976) Suggested that within the "Teddy Boy" **subculture** of the 1950s, status could be gained by the particular style of clothes worn.

Jones (1986) **Pluralist** who studied coverage of industrial disputes in the UK media. He argued that the radio generally reports both sides of industrial disputes; however, bias may occur if one side in the dispute is more successful in gaining media coverage for their views.

juvenile delinquency Any behaviour by young people who are under the age of legal responsibility that causes disruption. Includes serious crimes like burglary and non-criminal misbehaviour such as truanting from school.

Katz and Lazarsfeld (1955) Studied media influence on American voters' political opinions. They concluded that voting behaviour was generally not influenced directly by the media. However, voters were influenced by **opinion leaders**, who were themselves often influenced by the media. Their work led to the idea of the **two-step flow model**.

Kearney (1998) Suggested that the recent growth in numbers of girl gangs reflects wider changes in **gender roles**, with girls adopting more masculine behavioural patterns.

Keddie (1971) Argued that teachers classified students in terms of their perception of what they regarded as an "ideal student" — this was generally based on the middle class, top-stream student.

Kelly (1987) Studied links between **gender** and subject choice at school. Kelly argued that science was seen as a masculine subject for two main reasons: 1) because of the lack of female representation in science textbooks; 2) because girls were excluded in the classroom due to the more dominant behaviour of males.

Kerr and Siegel (1954) Came up with the **isolated mass theory** about the causes of strikes.

Keynes Economist who argued that **unemployment** is caused by low demand in the economy. He suggested that governments should increase spending in order to promote demand and thus decrease unemployment.

Kincaid (1973) Argued that **poverty** serves the interests of **capitalism** by providing a cheap labour supply, keeping wages low and preventing the working class from uniting. He was a **Marxist** — you'd never have guessed, would you.

kinship Relations based on birth, blood or adoption.

labelling theory Says the labels given to someone affect their behaviour, e.g. someone who's labelled a failure at school believes it and so *becomes* a failure at school. Labels also affect how others treat them, e.g.

17

teachers might expect trouble from a child who has been labelled "difficult", and therefore treat that child more strictly.

lab experiment   Piece of research carried out in a controlled environment. All the **variables** are controlled so that the effect of changing one variable can be measured. Compare with **field experiment**, **natural experiment**.

Labov (1973) Said that the speech codes used by working class pupils, recognised by **Bernstein**, reflected cultural differences, rather than being "restricted" or inferior to middle class speech codes.

Laing   Psychiatrist who believed that **mental illness**, such as schizophrenia, is a normal response to the negative pressures of family life and difficult relationships. He thought that mental breakdowns could lead to mental breakthroughs.

Lane and Roberts (1971) Argued that **strikes** that were supposedly about wages were often really about worker resentment to the authority of management.

Lash and Urry (1993) **Postmodernists** who suggested that advances in satellite, cable and Internet technology and the **globalisation** of culture have made **leisure** more individualised or "privatised". People are less likely to take part in group leisure activities such as football, and are more likely to seek their leisure at home through technology.

Laslett (1972) Argued that **nuclear families** existed before **industrialisation**, and that early industrialisation promoted the development of the **extended family**.

Lea and Young (1984) **Left Realists** who argued that inner city crime occurs because working class and black youth feels economically, socially and politically marginalised and deprived in comparison to middle class and white youth. They suggested that this leads some young people to look for status in **subcultures** (compare with **Willis**). Some subcultures are positive, e.g. sports clubs, others are negative, promoting delinquent behaviour including crime.

Lees (1986) Studied **gender** socialisation and found that the girls in her study conformed to gender expectations of being interested in love rather than sex. Lees said that this was to ensure that their reputations were protected.

Left Realism   Sociological viewpoint which developed from **Marxism**. The approach focuses on working within the capitalist framework and aims to direct **social policy** to help the poor. See **Lea and Young**.

Le Grand (1982, 2003) Suggested that the middle class get far more benefit from free **welfare** services, such as education and the NHS, than the working class do. Middle class children are more likely to stay on in education and are more likely to go to university compared to working class children who often leave education with few qualifications.

leisure   Any time left over after work-related and physiological activities (e.g. eating, sleeping). According to **Parker**, the type of work you do shapes your attitude to work and leisure:

- **extension pattern**   For professionals who have high job satisfaction, work and leisure are closely linked, with no clear boundary, e.g. taking clients to lunch.
- **neutrality pattern**   For semi-skilled and clerical workers who do not experience job satisfaction, there is a clear boundary between work and leisure. Leisure tends to be focused around the home and family.
- **oppositional pattern**   For unskilled manual workers who do not experience job satisfaction, there is a very clear distinction between work and leisure. Leisure activities such as drinking with workmates are of central importance and compensate for hard work.

Lewis (1959, 1961, 1966) Argued that culture was the cause of **poverty**, because the poor have their own **values**, **norms** and behaviour, e.g. they desire **immediate gratification**. Lewis said that the poor pass on these attitudes to the next generation, who learn how to be poor and so expect to be poor. Compare with **Coates and Silburn**.

libel laws These make it illegal to publish defamatory material in permanent form, e.g. in a written or printed statement or a drawing.

life space How people spend their time. **Parker** defined five types of life space:
* **work** Time spent in paid employment.
* **work obligations** E.g. Commuting to work.
* **non-work obligations** E.g. Childcare, housework.
* **physiological obligations** Time spent washing, eating, sleeping etc.
* **leisure** The time left over.

longitudinal study A study which is done at regular intervals over a long period of time on the same group of people.

Lull (1990) Suggested that different genders and age groups have different social needs and use the TV in different ways to meet these needs. See **uses and gratifications theory**.

McKeown (1976) Favoured the **social model of health**. McKeown argued that external (i.e. social) factors have been the main cause of poor health in the past, and that the general health of the public improved in the 19th century due to things like better sewage disposal, access to clean water, etc. These improvements occurred before the medical elite came to dominate health care, and McKeown therefore argues that today's improved health has little to do with medical intervention.

McQuail (1972) Studied soap opera audiences, and found that people watched *Coronation Street* to fulfil a need for social companionship. He concluded that audiences use the media to meet their own needs. See **uses and gratifications theory**.

McRobbie (1976, 1991) Claimed that teenage magazines aimed at girls reinforce conventional cultural notions of **femininity**, e.g. by running articles on how to get a boyfriend.

McRobbie and Garber (1976) Studied the **bedroom subculture** of teenage girls. They argued that female subcultures are not as publicly visible as male subcultures, due to the different cultural and behavioural expectations society has about girls.

Mac an Ghaill (1994) Used overt **observation** and **interviews** to study **masculinity**. He found that many boys formed **deviant subcultures** because of failure at school and a desire to be "macho" and masculine. He introduced the idea of a "crisis of masculinity" as a cause of the underachievement of boys at school.

Mack and Lansley (1985, 1992) Compiled a "deprivation index" of items essential to social life, based on a survey of the general public. They concluded that relative poverty was still a significant problem in the UK in the 1980s and 1990s.

Maduro (1982) Neo-**Marxist** who argued that religion is both a product and a source of social conflict. Therefore it isn't always a conservative force in society, and can even bring about social **revolution**.

Malinowski (1954) **Functionalist** who carried out anthropological research on the Trobriand islanders in Papua New Guinea. He concluded that religion provided the people with stability during unpredictable or stressful events, like births and deaths, which would otherwise threaten social order.

Marcuse (1964) Neo-**Marxist** who wrote about **leisure**, its consumption by workers and the way it is presented by the **mass media**. He claimed that the mass media promotes consumerism and gives people **false needs** (things they think they want but which won't really satisfy them). He said that leisure is based around these false needs, creating "happy robots" who work hard because they're under the false impression that leisure makes them happy.

marginalisation When a group or individual is pushed to the edges of mainstream society — their needs and concerns are treated as unimportant by the government, education system, mass media etc.

market situation Concept used by **Weberian** sociologists to explain wealth distribution. Market situation refers to how valuable and scarce an individual's skills are in society. For example, plumbers are currently in short supply in the UK, so there is a lot of demand for their skills. This means that they have a good market situation and can demand higher wages.

Marsland (1989) **New Right** theorist who argued that all universal **benefits** should be abolished because they encourage dependency, which he claimed ultimately makes people poorer. He felt that benefits should only exist for the very poorest people and for the shortest possible time.

Marxism A school of thought based on the views of Karl Marx (1818-1883). Marxists are opposed to **capitalism**, which they believe is

Karl Marx

based on the exploitation of the working class (proletariat) by the owning class (bourgeoisie). Marxists also tend to be opposed to **religion,** believing that it serves to create a **false consciousness**. Marxists believe that people's identity is socially created, based on their **class** and position in capitalist society. They study how aspects of society's **superstructure** — e.g. education, the media, religion — serve to reinforce existing class divisions and perpetuate capitalism.

- **Neo-Marxism** In the 20th century, some of Marx's followers revised and adapted his ideas to make them more relevant to contemporary society and to correct mistakes they perceived in traditional Marxism. Neo-Marxist analysis of capitalist society tends to be more subtle and complex than traditional Marxist analysis. Neo-Marxists stress the importance of the role of **culture** in sustaining capitalism, for example through the **hegemony** of capitalist ideas.

masculinity Socially constructed ideas of how men should look and behave. See **Rutherford, Mac an Ghaill**.

mass media All the ways of communicating with large numbers of people, including newspapers, films, TV and radio.

master status Refers to a quality in an individual that comes to dominate the way that they are treated or viewed, to the extent that all their other qualities are disregarded. This quality then takes on the status of a label. For example, a person with mental health problems might be given the often negative label of "mentally ill", and find that all their other qualities are then ignored. The label "mentally ill" then has master status.

material deprivation Lack of the basic material things considered necessary for living, e.g. money, decent living conditions. See **Douglas, Halsey**.

mechanisation The use of machinery to replace human labour. A feature of assembly line production — see **Braverman, deskilling**.

media messages Media messages go through four stages from production to end effect, a process referred to by sociologists as the process of message trajectory. The four stages are:
1) media message is formulated by editors
2) media content reflects groups in power
3) message is received by the audience
4) message affects social behaviour and opinions
See **Cumberbatch, Hermes, Ferguson, McRobbie, Tuchman, Wolf**.

media text A piece of media, e.g. a newspaper article, an advert, a TV programme.

medical elite   Medical professionals, seen by the **biomedical model of health** as the only people sufficiently qualified to identify and treat illness.

medicalisation of childbirth   Identified by **Oakley** as the process by which women's control over childbirth has been taken away by the medical profession. Pregnancy is equated with illness and pregnant women are treated as patients.

Melton (1993) Disagreed with the Interactionist view that **New Religious Movements** emerge in periods of uncertainty. Melton traced the origin of many American New Religious Movements to the 1950s, a period of stability and certainty for the USA.

mental illness   This can be seen as a biomedical condition to be treated and cured, for example with drugs. But another view of mental illness has developed, which treats mental health problems as **social constructs**. Sociologists have examined the social causes of mental illness from a variety of sociological perspectives, e.g. **Marxist, feminist, Interactionist**. For example, feminists like **Busfield** and **Nicolson** see women's mental illness as a result of patriarchy. See also **Goffman, Szasz**.

meritocracy   A system where the most talented and hard-working people rise to the top. In such a system, educational and social success is the result of ability combined with effort.

message trajectory   The process of **media messages** reaching their audience.

middle class   People who earn their money from non-manual work. Compare with **upper class, working class, underclass**.

Miliband (1969) **Marxist** sociologist who wrote extensively about the role of the State and the **mass media** in capitalist society. He claimed that the mass media encourages the **proletariat** to be subordinate and happy to serve the **bourgeoisie**.

millenarianism   A type of **New Religious Movement** based on a belief in an imminent apocalyptic event through which its members will achieve salvation, e.g. the return of the Messiah.

Miller (1962) Studied delinquent **subcultures**. He disagreed with Albert **Cohen**'s view that working class deviant behaviour is a reaction to the inability of working class groups to achieve success. Instead he claimed that there is a distinct working class culture, with its own **norms** and **values** that are completely different to those of middle class culture.

Mirza (1992) Studied how **ethnicity** affects achievement in school. Mirza found that the black girls she studied had positive self-esteem, high aspirations and strategies to deal with **racism**. Mirza believed that the reason some of the girls underachieved was because they were unwilling to ask for help or unwilling to choose certain subjects.

Mitsos and Browne (1998) Studied the question of why girls now do better than boys at school. They claimed that this is partly due to the "feminisation of teaching" (i.e. the increase in numbers of female teachers), which makes doing well at school seem **feminine** and therefore unappealing to boys. They also suggested that boys lose valuable learning time due to their own misbehaviour in class and their much higher chance of being excluded from school.

Modood et al. (1997) Studied how **ethnicity** is related to **family structure**, e.g. they found that whites and Afro-Caribbeans were generally more likely than Asians to be divorced. They also looked at educational achievement, finding that some ethnic minorities were more likely to go into further education than white people.

moral panic   When media exaggeration creates a strong negative public reaction to a social group or phenomenon. Term first used by Stan **Cohen**.

Morgan (1975) Sociologist who criticised **Murdock** for idealising the universal nuclear family and ignoring negative aspects of family life. Morgan pointed out that Murdock made no reference to alternative households or to disharmony and problems in family relationships.

Morley (1980) Sociologist who studied audience responses to a then popular early evening news and current affairs programme called *Nationwide*. He found that responses varied according to social group — each group thought the programme was biased against them. So I suppose he also found that people tend to be rather paranoid. See **structured interpretation model**.

mortification of the self The processes used, especially in total institutions like prisons and psychiatric hospitals, to take away individuals' liberty and privacy and to make them conform. **Goffman** used the term to describe the techniques used by the psychiatric staff he studied, and claimed that it leads to the patient losing their identity.

Murdock (1949) **Functionalist** sociologist who identified four basic functions of the **nuclear family** — sexual, reproductive, economic and educational. Murdock considered these functions to be so important that he thought some form of the nuclear family would always exist in all cultures — the universal nuclear family.

Murray (1989, 1993, 1995) **New Right** sociologist who argued that **welfare** benefits were putting the traditional family under threat because they created an **underclass** with a "**culture of dependency**". He recommended a "moral" benefits system to discourage the growth of single parent families. He believed that unmarried women with children should get no benefits at all.

National Curriculum A range of compulsory subjects that all 5 to 16 year olds must study at school in the UK. Introduced as part of the 1988 Education Reform Act.

National Health Service (NHS) The system of public healthcare provided by the government for all UK citizens. Set up in 1947 with the aim of providing free and equal health care for everyone in the UK.

national identity The feeling that you belong to a country and its people.

national ritual Ceremonial events which contribute to a feeling of national identity, e.g. Remembrance Sunday, State Opening of Parliament. Often highlighted by the media.

natural experiment An experiment that is not set up artificially, e.g. **twin studies**. Compare with **field experiment**, **lab experiment**.

Navarro (1976) **Marxist** sociologist noted for his critique of the role of the NHS in capitalist society. He claimed that the NHS and **medical elite** play an ideological role, drawing attention away from the social and environmental causes of disease. Compare with **Gough**.

neo-tribe **Bennett**'s term for a group that is loosely and temporarily connected by fashion and lifestyle. It has been suggested that neo-tribes are a modern phenomenon lacking the shared values of earlier **subcultures**, and therefore usually lacking their longevity and cohesion.

New Age Movement A term which encompasses the range of religions and therapies which have grown in importance since the 1970s, e.g. feng shui, aromatherapy, astrology. New Age beliefs appeal to people who have turned away from traditional religion. The New Age Movement encourages people to find salvation, peace or perfection inside themselves — the philosophy is quite individualistic, and there is little overall organisation or authority. See **Bruce**, **Heelas**.

New Religious Movement (NRM) Any form of religious movement that has grown in popularity in recent times. Used by some sociologists as evidence of the continuing importance of religion in social life. See **Bruce, Wallis**.

New Right Movement developed in the 1980s. New Right theory believes in the "moral superiority" of the traditional **nuclear family**, and tends towards the view that sexual tolerance and single mothers are bad for society. Problems like poverty and unemployment are seen to be caused by an over-generous **welfare state**. New Right sociologists have also claimed that there's been a moral decline in society due to **secularisation**. See **Marsland**, **Murray**.

news values The rules and ideas that journalists follow, believing that they represent what the public wants to hear about. News values can vary depending on the type of programme/publication a journalist is working for.
- **bureaucratic news values** Belief that news should be current, simple and brief. Big news is better than small news.
- **cultural news values** Belief that news should be unexpected, focus on important people and be relevant to the audience. Bad news is better than good news.

New Welfare Contract New Labour policy introduced in 1998. It stated that the government will help people to find work, help with childcare and support the poorest old people and those who can't work, but that people also have to take individual responsibility, e.g. by saving for their retirements, etc.

Nicolson (1998) Feminist sociologist who studied post-natal depression. Nicolson argued that it is a social rather than a physical condition. She said that post-natal depression isn't a mental disorder, and that it's natural to feel depressed after giving birth.

norm A social rule about what is correct or appropriate behaviour within a particular culture, e.g. queueing in a shop.

NS-SEC Stands for National Statistics Socio-Economic Classification. It is a way of defining social stratification used in the UK Census. It divides people into eight classes based on the jobs they do.

nuclear family A family made up of parents and their dependent children. Seen by many sociologists as a product of **industrialisation**. Compare with **extended family**.

Oakley Feminist sociologist noted for her in-depth critique of the notion of symmetrical conjugal roles in the household. Oakley argued that women in fact now have a "double burden", taking on paid work in addition to doing most of the housework and childcare. She felt that the role of the housewife was socially constructed after **industrialisation**. She identified four types of **gender socialisation** in family life:
- **canalisation** Children are given toys that channel their interest in a certain direction, e.g. toy guns for boys, dolls for girls. Children therefore come to learn that some activities are considered appropriate for boys and others are appropriate for girls.
- **different activities** Involving boys and girls in different aspects of the household. For instance, household chores are often allocated to children on the basis of their sex. "Normal" behaviour for men and women is therefore established in the mind of the child.
- **manipulation** "Normal" behaviour is encouraged and **deviant** behaviour is discouraged, manipulating the child's self-image. Typically, parents spend greater amounts of time "manipulating" girls than they do boys, e.g. stressing the importance of appearance, etc.
- **verbal appellation** The language and names used to describe the child. For example, praising a girl on her pretty appearance rewards the child and teaches her that she must continue this behaviour to earn social approval. This reinforces ideas about gender roles.

observation Primary research that involves watching social behaviour in real-life settings.

Favoured by **interactionists** as it produces valid **qualitative data**.

- **covert observation**   The researcher doesn't tell the group they're being observed.
- **overt observation**   The group is aware of the research and who the researcher is.
- **non-participant observation**   The researcher observes the group but doesn't become an active member of it.
- **participant observation**   The researcher becomes an active member of the group he/she is studying.

Ofcom   Government office that regulates and monitors the UK communications industry (the media). It was set up in January 2004. It deals with complaints and can fine or close down those that break the rules.

Ofsted   The Office for Standards in Education — government office that inspects schools and standards of education. Set up in 1993.

open-ended question   A question without a list of options to choose from, leaving the respondent free to answer how they see fit — e.g. "How do you feel about the area where you live?" Favoured by **Interactionists**, as they tend to produce valid **qualitative data**.

opinion leader   A key individual in a community who openly expresses his/her opinions, influencing the actions and opinions of others. **Katz and Lazarsfeld** said opinion leaders often get their opinions straight from the mass media.

Orbach (1991) Feminist psychotherapist who agreed with **Wolf** that media messages about how women should look are responsible for a rise in eating disorders.

Pahl (1984, 1989, 1993) Conducted research on husbands and wives concerning who tends to make the decisions about money. She found the most common form was "husband controlled pooling", where the couple's earnings are shared but the man has the final say on how it's spent. Pahl concluded that women still had some way to go in terms of equality in money management within the family.

Parker (1976) Defined five categories of **life space**, and suggested that the type of work an individual does affects how they spend their **leisure**.

Parsons   American **functionalist** sociologist who believed the family has two main roles: the primary **socialisation** of children and the stabilisation of adult personalities. He also believed in the importance to society of schools, as they act as a bridge between the family and society for young people. He said that schools also have a role in selecting individuals for their future roles in society. N.B. His first name is Talcott and in the weird world of Sociology, he is very famous indeed.

patriarchy   The combination of systems, **ideologies** and cultural practices in all parts of society which ensure that men have power and authority over women.

peer group People of the same or similar social status and age, e.g. a group of teenagers.

peripheral worker   A low paid, temporary worker who lacks job security.

Phillips (2003) Journalist who criticised radical **feminist** theories about domestic violence. She pointed out that women abuse men too and male victims are often ignored by society and the police.

Piachaud (1981, 1987) Criticised **Townsend**'s deprivation index, arguing that it reflected Townsend's own ideas concerning what should be considered necessities.

pilot study   A small-scale piece of research which reflects the main study. It is used as a trial run to work out costs and to iron out any potential problems before carrying out the actual research.

Pluralism   The theory that society is diverse and so reflects the needs and views of everyone, e.g. if one part of the media is **biased** one way, another will be biased the other way, thus catering for all views and creating a balanced picture overall.

Pollert (1988) Argued that **neo-Fordist** companies use **peripheral workers** in order to maximise profits by reducing costs. Used the term "coercive pacification" to refer to the use of a peripheral workforce to weaken trade unions and reduce industrial conflict.

Positivism   Argues that human behaviour is determined by external social factors, and so is outside the control of the individuals in society. Positivists believe that sociology should be a science based on learning more about these external forces that control behaviour. Positivist research therefore looks for cause and effect relationships, using **questionnaires** and official statistics to obtain **quantitative data**.

Postmodernism   Theory that says there is no one objective truth or reality that everyone experiences. People are able to make their own decisions about who they are and how they live their lives. In a postmodern society, **media messages** are increasingly important in constructing one's identity. For example, people buy designer clothes because they convey an image which has been transmitted by the media. See **Baudrillard**.

poverty   Living in deprived conditions. Sociologists disagree about exactly how to define poverty.
*   **absolute poverty**   Not having enough income to afford the basic necessities — food, warmth and shelter.
*   **relative poverty**   Being relatively deprived, in comparison to other people in the same society. For example, not being able to afford a TV if owning one in that society is regarded as normal.

preferred reading   A dominant interpretation of a **media text**, influenced by the social context of the text. Implies that the way we interpret a media text depends on the cultural attitudes of the time.

Press Complaints Commission (PCC)   Set up by the press to monitor standards and deal with complaints.

primary data   Data collected by first hand research and obtained through methods such as **interviews** and **questionnaires**.

principles of stratification   Functionalist theory of stratification described by **Davis and Moore** which suggests that in order for a society to survive, there must be a system of effective role allocation. The education system is seen as the means of selecting people based on their ability and motivation.

proletariat   **Marxist** term for the working class who sell their labour for wages.

qualitative data   In-depth data that is concerned with the meanings and interpretations people give to issues and events. Qualitative data is generally small-scale, and it can be difficult to draw wider conclusions from it.

quantitative data   Data that can be expressed in numerical or statistical form, enabling comparisons over time to be made. Quantitative data is often large-scale but it tends to lack detail.

questionnaire   A printed list of questions which is either filled out by the respondent or by the researcher asking the questions.
*   **standardised questionnaire**   Asks the same closed questions to everyone taking part.

racism   Belief or action that treats one ethnic group as inferior to another.

Rastafarianism   A religious and political movement founded by Marcus Garvey that originated in Jamaica and is based around black resistance to white dominance. Some of the movement's features have been adopted by young black people in Britain, who expressed their dissatisfaction with racism and unemployment by forming a **subculture** based around Rastafarianism.

reliability   Research is reliable if other sociologists using the same methods on the same group collect the same data. **Quantitative data** is usually the most reliable.

religion   An organised system of spiritual or supernatural beliefs followed by a number of people.

religious pluralism   Many different religious groups and beliefs being present in a society.

representative data   This means that the sample of the population studied to generate the data reflects the characteristics of the population as a whole (e.g. the proportions of different age groups and genders is the same).

revolution   A political revolution is the overthrow and replacement of one ruling system by another. The word "revolution" can also be used to describe sudden and/or large-scale changes to the economy or social structure.

rite of passage   A significant event that marks a change in someone's life. Sometimes rites of passage are marked by a ceremony, e.g. a baptism or a wedding.

Roberts (1978) Argued that people are free to choose from the variety of **leisure** patterns available in society. He disagreed with the **Marxist** view that leisure is imposed on consumers, arguing instead that the leisure industry has to respond to public demand in order to make a profit.

role   The expectations society has about the behaviour and actions of an individual, based on their **status**.

Rowntree (1901, 1941, 1951) Conducted the first major study of absolute **poverty** in the UK. It was based on how many families could afford

a list of "essential" basic items needed for life, such as food, shelter and warmth.

Rutherford (1998) Studied how the media's representation of men is changing. Rutherford pointed out that men in the media are now being portrayed in traditionally female ways, e.g. male stripper groups as sex objects. Rutherford concluded that there's been a **feminisation of masculinity**.

sample A selection of people used for a survey.
- **quota sample**   Picking only people who fit into a certain category, e.g. age group.
- **simple random sample**   Picking names randomly from a list.
- **snowball sample**   Finding an initial contact who gives you more names.
- **stratified sample**   Dividing the population into groups (e.g. by gender), and taking a random selection with the correct proportions (e.g. if 60% of the population is male, then 60% of the sample should be male).

Schudson (1994) Argued that people are socialised into a national culture and identity by things like education (e.g. teaching of national history) and the **mass media** (e.g. coverage of royal events).

scientific management   System of management devised by **Taylor**, based on a division of labour where each worker carries out one low-skilled task all the time. This is the theory that **Fordism** put into practice.

Scott (1980, 1990) Argued that the **upper class** use the public school system to create social networks which lead onto many of the best jobs. He also warned of the dangers of sociologists analysing **secondary data**, saying it might not be authentic, credible or representative, and may reflect the subjective interpretation of the author.

Scraton (1994) Feminist sociologist who said that women's **leisure** opportunities are still largely shaped by:

1) a relative lack of disposable income, because women are often in part-time rather than full-time employment, or are not employed at all.

2) societal expectations of **gender roles**. Women still tend to have most of the childcare responsibilities and to do most of the housework, so they have less time available for leisure.

secondary data   Existing information that you gather and analyse but which has already been generated, e.g. official statistics, letters, newspapers.

sect   A small, radical religious movement. Often formed by people who are dissatisfied with the teachings of a mainstream church.

secularisation   When religion loses its influence over society.   Secularisation is thought to be caused by the social changes brought about by **industrialisation** and the development of scientific knowledge.

selective filter model   Argues that an audience chooses which parts of the mass media they experience. They can pick out parts of a **media message** which fit in with their view of the world and ignore the rest. This model emphasises the power of the individual to control his/her experience of the media and says that people use the media in a sophisticated way. See **Fiske**.

self-fulfilling prophecy   When someone is labelled in a particular way, and as a result they turn out that way. For example, the "self-fulfilling prophecy of educational failure" suggests that students who are labelled and treated as failures at school will end up failures because of that label. See **labelling theory**.

Sharpe (1976, 1994) Conducted a study which showed that teenage girls' attitudes had changed over time, which is why they now do better at school. In the 1970s, they mostly valued marriage and motherhood. In the 1990s, they stressed their career ambitions.

Signorelli (1989) Studied age **stereotypes** on American TV and found that both young and old people were under-represented — TV was biased towards middle-aged people.

situational constraints theory   Says that the poor are constrained by their situation (e.g. low income, poor housing, unemployment), not by their attitudes or values — so poverty is practically hard to get out of, rather than culturally hard to get out of. See **Coates and Silburn**.

Smith (1987) Author of the book *Different for Girls*, which argued that culture creates and perpetuates gender differences. Smith claimed that men and women are treated differently by society and so they become different.

social construct   An attitude or idea that is created by society rather than based on objective facts.   For example, gender differences may be based on society's ideas about how men and women should behave, rather than on the biological difference between them.

social democratic theory   Suggests that institutions in society are the cause of poverty. Social democrats believe in increasing **welfare** provision (such as benefits), in order to re-distribute wealth and resources from rich to poor.

social determinism   Says social forces determine how technology develops and people choose how to react to it.   Compare **technological determinism**.

social model of health   Focuses on the external causes of illness, i.e. the social and environmental factors, such as poor diet or poor housing. Compare with the **biomedical model of health**.

social policy   Government decisions that affect society, e.g. raising taxes, changing the benefits system, changing divorce laws.

social survey   Used to collect information about a large group of people, usually using standardised **questionnaires** or structured **interviews**.

S

Social Trends   A collection of regular UK government surveys published every year which show current trends in society, e.g. a rise in cohabitation rates or in the number of people employed part-time.

socialisation   Passing on cultural **values** and **norms** from one generation to the next, so that they become internalised, i.e. part of everyone's way of thinking.
- **primary socialisation**   Young children learn the skills, knowledge, norms and values of society from their parents/ guardians to enable them to fit into society. They're rewarded for socially acceptable behaviour and punished for **deviance**.
- **secondary socialisation**   This builds on primary socialisation throughout a person's life. There are many agents of secondary socialisation, such as school, **religion**, **peer groups** and the **mass media**.

socialism   An economic system based on public ownership and common welfare. Production is for the good of society rather than for profit. Compare with **capitalism**.

Spencer   19th Century sociologist who said that the poor were those in society who had failed to do the best for themselves, because they're immoral and lazy. He felt that the State should interfere as little as possible, because it was poor people's own fault that they were poor.

Spender (1983) Studied the question of why girls used to underachieve at school, saying that education was controlled and dominated by men. Spender argued that the curriculum was male-centred and involved little reference to female contributions to the development of society. She also felt that boys were given more of the teacher's attention than girls in the classroom, and that this was to prepare girls for their lower status role in society as housewives and mothers.

spiritual shopper   Someone who samples different religious movements to find the "best fit".

Stacey (1990) **Postmodernist** sociologist who argued that there's such a diversity of family types that there'll never be one dominant type of family in Western culture again.

Stanworth (1983) Suggested that girls used to underachieve at school because teachers held stereotypical views about what girls would do in the future (e.g. marriage and children rather than careers).   This meant that girls were disadvantaged in the classroom because they got less attention from the teachers, were often negatively labelled and received little encouragement to succeed academically.

statistics   A set of figures showing the results of research — a way of showing **quantitative data**. Official statistics are produced by local or central government or government agencies.
- **hard statistics**   Objective statistics where there's one simple way of measuring them, e.g. births and marriages.
- **soft statistics**   Where the method of measuring them can change depending on the definition used, e.g. crime, poverty, unemployment.

status   An individual's position in a **hierarchy**, in terms of the amount of social importance, respect and recognition that they are given by other members of society.
- **achieved status**   Social status that's been earned through education and work, e.g. headteacher.
- **ascribed status**   Social status that you're born into, e.g. Queen.

stereotype   A generalisation about a certain type of person, e.g. "all football supporters are hooligans." Often inaccurate and negative.

stratification   The division of the members of society into a hierarchy of different status groups, e.g. upper class, middle class and working class.

strike   When workers organise themselves and collectively stop working until a grievance is addressed by management or owners. Strikes are often the result of **trade union** activity. See

Edwards and Scullion, Kerr and Siegel and Lane and Roberts for possible reasons for strikes.

structural theory   Sociological viewpoint that argues that human attitudes and behaviour are determined by the big structures in society, e.g. the way production is run.   **Functionalism** and **Marxism** are structural theories.   Compare to **action theory**.

structure of society   The way society is organised and operates as a whole.

structured interpretation model   Suggests that different social groups have different ways of interpreting **media messages** from the same programmes or articles. For example, one group may see a programme as biased, another may think the same programme is harmlessly entertaining, and yet another group might see it as boring. See **Morley**.

subculture   A group with shared **values** and **norms** that breaks away from mainstream culture, for example youth subcultures.
- **spectacular subculture**   Dramatic subculture that attracts the attention of the public and **mass media** by dressing flamboyantly and often breaking the norms of society, e.g. Punks.

Sugarman (1970) Suggested that middle class and working class children are socialised into different **norms** and **values** — middle class children are encouraged to plan for **deferred gratification**, whereas working class children go for **immediate gratification**.

superstructure   In **Marxist** theory, the superstructure is the major institutions in a society which aren't economic (such as the legal and political systems) plus the system of beliefs and values of the society. Marxists believe that the superstructure is shaped by the **infrastructure** (the economic base of society), but it also has a role in maintaining and sustaining the infrastructure.   So, the infrastructure and superstructure have a two-way relationship — they need each other. Ahhh, this Marxist theory is so sweet.

Swann Report (1985) Found that there were differences in educational achievement between ethnic minority groups, with Pakistani, Bangladeshi and Afro-Caribbean pupils doing less well compared with other ethnic groups. The report concluded that socio-economic factors were the main cause of Afro-Caribbean pupils' underachievement.

symbolic creativity   When young people actively create their own individual styles by mixing up whatever is available to them, e.g. using religious crosses as fashion items. Described by **Willis**.

symmetrical family   Where husband and wife have fairly equal **conjugal roles**, with the male partner taking responsibility for close to half of the domestic work and childcare. See **Willmott and Young**.

Szasz (1971) Interactionist who suggested that **mental illness** was just a **social construct** used to control non-conformist behaviour. He argued that people should be free to choose whether to get psychotherapy or not, and his name is rather hard to pronounce.

Taylor   Used time and motion studies to come up with the concept of **scientific management**, which gives management greater control of the workforce.

technological determinism   Suggests that technology is an independent force which affects people and organisation of work. For example, car assembly lines control the speed at which employees work. Compare with **social determinism**.

third way politics   New Labour's style of combining the social policies of old Labour, which promoted social equality, with the more right wing policies of the Conservatives.

Thompson (1989) Argued against the **post-Fordist** view that modern mass production requires skilled, flexible workers. He viewed mass production from a **neo-Fordist** perspective — workers are trained to multi-task so that they can perform any low skilled, repetitive task (e.g. on a production line or in a fast food restaurant).

Thrasher (1927) American sociologist who argued that gangs were an important part of **socialisation** in all poor communities.

Townsend (1970, 1979) Studied relative **poverty** in the UK, using a "deprivation index" of items he saw as essential to social life. He argued that to be without these items was to be living in poverty. The main cause of poverty as Townsend saw it was the inadequate level of benefits that workers were reliant on. He also suggested that because of their low incomes, the poor experienced low status which prevented them improving their **market situation**. Townsend believed that the best way of improving standards of living was through the **Welfare State**. See **Piachaud**.

trade union An organisation of workers centred around a particular trade that negotiates on behalf of its members, e.g. National Union of Teachers.

triangulation Combining different methods or types of data for the same piece of research — e.g. using **questionnaires** and overt participant **observation**. This is useful because each method has different strengths and weaknesses. Combining quantitative and qualitative methods gives more detailed data than if only one method is used.

tripartite system Schools system introduced by the 1944 Education Act, in which pupils were selected for one of three types of school based on their performance in the 11+ exam. See **Butler Act**.

Troeltsch (1912) Studied religious organisations. He said churches have four main features:
1) They claim a monopoly over the truth.
2) They have a complex, rigid hierarchy and bureaucratic structure.
3) They have a close relationship with the state — for example, the Queen is the head of state and head of the Church of England.
4) They are integrated into mainstream society, acting as a conservative force.

Tuchman (1978) Studied media **stereotypes** of women. Concluded there were only two narrow female roles portrayed in the media: domestic and sexual.

Tudor Hart (1971) Concluded that an **inverse care law** operated within the National Health Service. Those most in need of health care (the poor) received fewer or less effective resources than those with less need (the middle classes).

Turkle (1996) **Postmodernist** who said that people can relate to a simulated world as easily as reality. Turkle claimed that what we see on television often becomes part of our world; for example, characters from soap operas are seen as real people rather than as actors playing a role.

twin study An experiment where identical twins are studied in different situations. This kind of study can be used to investigate whether something is caused by genetics or by **socialisation**.

two-step flow model Argues that not everyone is influenced directly by the media. In the first step, the media message reaches an audience member. In the second step, the audience's understanding of the message is shaped by social interaction, most notably with those people whose views they respect (**opinion leaders**). See **Katz and Lazarsfeld**.

underclass A group of people at the bottom of the social structure who rely on **welfare benefits**

for income, and who are excluded from wider society because they are living in **poverty**. Includes the long-term unemployed, some elderly people, some single-parent families and the homeless. Compare with **upper class**, **middle class**, **working class**.

unemployment   The amount of people who do not have a job. There are various ways of measuring unemployment.
- **cyclical unemployment**   This describes how unemployment fluctuates according to the strength of the economy.
- **frictional unemployment**   People who lose their jobs then quickly get new ones, and who are therefore only unemployed for a short time.
- **structural unemployment**   When either a group of workers' skills are no longer required by society (e.g. miners), or when people are unemployed because they live in an area where there are no jobs that require their skills.

upper class   The wealthiest and most powerful people in society, who pass on their wealth and power from one generation to the next. Compare with **middle class**, **working class**, **underclass**.

uses and gratifications theory   Functionalist theory developed by **Blumler and Katz** (1974). They suggested that different people use the media in different ways to meet their various needs, e.g. the need for companionship. See **Lull**, **McQuail**.

validity   Research is valid if it gives a true and detailed picture of what is being measured.

value   A general belief in a society about what is important or what is right and wrong, e.g. freedom of speech is a value of western society.

Van Dijk (1991) Analysed ethnic **stereotypes** in British newspaper headlines. He found that negative images far outweighed positive ones, e.g. the focus of press coverage about black people tended to be on the negative issues of crime and violence.

variable   Something that is tested or measured in an experiment. The researcher changes the independent variable and observes the effect on the dependent variable.

verstehen   Weber's term for when a researcher uses empathy to work out why someone does or says something. To understand why people act in a certain way (e.g. commit crime), you have to try and understand their motives (e.g. living in poverty). To do this, you have to imagine yourself in their position. This idea is central to **Interactionism**.

vocational education   Courses aimed at providing students with more specific work-related skills needed by industry, e.g. the new vocational A-levels in Business Studies.

Walker and Walker (1994) Argued in favour of an "active employment strategy", where the government would create work for the unemployed and reduce social exclusion.

Wallis (1984) Sociologist who identified three types of **New Religious Movement**:
- **world-accommodating movements**   Try to rediscover spiritual purity in traditional religions, e.g. Pentacostalism.
- **world-affirming movements**   Try to "unlock spiritual power" to enable followers to be more successful in society, e.g. transcendental meditation.
- **world-rejecting movements**   Cut themselves off from society and demand total commitment from members, e.g. the Unification Church ("Moonies").

wealth   The value of all an individual's possessions minus debts.
- **marketable wealth**   Possessions that can be sold, e.g. clothes, jewellery, property, shares.
- **non-marketable wealth**   Finance-based things like a salary or pension fund.

Weber (b.1864 d.1920) Early sociologist who wrote *The Protestant Ethic and the Spirit of Capitalism*. Weber argued that the better a person's **market situation**, the better their life-chances, wealth and status would be — that is, the more demand there is in a society for particular skills, the more easily a person with those skills can gain a high salary and social standing. He also suggested that as societies developed, **secularisation** would follow as people came to believe more in scientific explanations and less in God and religion.

Weberians Followers of the work and ideas of Max **Weber**.

welfare provision In the UK there are four sectors of welfare provision:
- **public sector** State services funded by tax and national insurance, e.g. a largely free NHS, a compulsory, free education system, a range of social services and the **benefits** system.
- **private sector** Services run by companies for profit and paid for directly by the individual, e.g. private hospitals, public schools, nurseries. They have to meet state regulations.
- **voluntary sector** Charities like hospices and Help the Aged. They provide services for free or at a state-subsided low cost, and are not run to make a profit. They also have to meet state regulations.
- **informal sector** Provided by individuals, often friends and family, when there isn't enough state provision, e.g. family carers, childminders. There's little or no state funding or regulation.

Welfare State The British Welfare State was set up in the 1940s after the publication of the Beveridge Report. Its aim was to wipe out the social problems of society (poor health, housing and education, poverty and unemployment). The Welfare State was designed to be free at the point where people actually needed it (e.g. a visit to hospital) and was paid for by people in work contributing to a national insurance scheme. During the 1980s, the Conservative government made many reforms to the Welfare State to reduce its size and costs (e.g. privatising some welfare provision, reducing universal benefits and increasing voluntary welfare provision). Under New Labour in the late 1990s and 2000s, there's been an emphasis on making the NHS and social security more efficient to save money.

Westergaard and Resler (1976) Marxists who argued that redistribution of wealth won't happen until capitalism is overthrown and replaced by a **socialist** society where wealth is communally owned.

Willis (1977, 1990) Argued that working class boys form anti-school **subcultures** because they associate school values with being "girly". He suggested that today there is no single dominant youth subculture because there's such a wide range of styles and tastes. He argued that young people don't want to join uniformed subcultures like the Teddy Boys or Punks any more. Instead they have a more individualistic approach, using **symbolic creativity** to make their own style.

Willmott and Young (1960, 1973) Studied British family structures. They found the family developed through three stages:
- **Stage 1: Pre-industrial** The family lives and works together. Work and home are combined. Families largely produce for their own needs. **Nuclear family** was the most common form.
- **Stage 2: Early industrial** Men leave home to work and women are left at home to do the housework and take care of the children. **Extended family** was the most common form.
- **Stage 3: Privatised nuclear** Modern **symmetrical family** based on consumption, not production, with men taking a more active role in home life. **Nuclear family** is the most common form.

Wilson (1966) Defined **secularisation** as a "process whereby religion loses its influence over the various spheres of social life".

Wolf (1990) Studied the effects of **media messages**. She said that the rise in eating disorders in women is a direct result of distorted and idealised media images of women's bodies. For example, women presented by the media as attractive tend to be very slim, and although for most women this is not a natural shape for their bodies to be, it is still promoted as the ideal woman.

work Activities people do because they get paid for them or because they have to do them (e.g. washing up) — work is not done primarily for pleasure. There has been a clearer distinction between work and **leisure** since **industrialisation**.

working class People who make their money from manual work. Compare with **upper class**, **middle class**, **underclass**.

work to rule A form of **industrial action** where workers only work to the letter of their contracts and refuse to perform any of their normal additional tasks in order to reduce efficiency and output.

Wright (1992) Studied ethnic prejudice inside schools. Wright found that, even though staff said they were committed to equal opportunities, Asian girls got less attention from teachers than white pupils, and Afro-Caribbean boys were more likely to be sent out of class because of teachers' assumptions about their behaviour.

Wright Mills (1951) Suggested office workers and sales people can suffer **alienation** because they have to put on a mask of being "nice" or "sincere" for customers and sometimes for other members of staff. They can't express their real emotions or show their real personalities to these people. Unless they really are nice and sincere, of course.

Zaretsky (1976) **Marxist** sociologist who argued that the family serves the needs of **capitalism** in three main ways:

1) The family relieves the alienation and frustration experienced by workers due to their lack of power in the workplace. Zaretsky said that when a working man goes home he's "king of his own castle," which makes it easier for him to accept his low **status** at work.
2) Capitalism requires a future workforce, which is produced and reared by women free of charge.
3) The family acts as a unit of consumption for capitalist goods.

Zimbalist (1979) Studied the print industry and found that **deskilling** occurred with the introduction of technology. When machines began to do a lot of the work that had previously been done by people, the workers no longer needed to be so skilled. Zimbalist argued that this made the workers easier to replace, and therefore easier to exploit. The fact that the skills of the workforce were no longer so important to management meant that the power of the **trade unions** was also reduced, which further increased the potential for exploitation.

Zuboff (1988) Studied the impact of technology on the workplace. She found that in some organisations, the introduction of technology meant that jobs that used to involve face-to-face skills were now done in front of a machine, so personal contact with customers and with other workers was lost. However, other organisations used technology to give workers greater freedom by increasing communication between them, e.g. through email.

The Individual and Society

This section helps you to revise particular topics. Check that you understand the key terms, concepts and studies listed for the topics you are studying. Then test yourself with the questions on each topic. *(The topic 'The Individual and Society' is for OCR, but is also useful for AQA.)*

Key Terms

- achieved status
- action theory
- ascribed status
- canalisation
- class
- conformity
- consensus
- constraint
- cultural capital
- culture
- deviance
- ethnicity
- femininity
- feminism
- Functionalism
- gender
- gender roles
- identity
- infrastructure
- Interactionism
- internalisation
- labelling theory
- leisure

- manipulation
- Marxism
- masculinity
- middle class
- national identity
- national ritual
- norm
- NS-SEC
- peer group
- Postmodernism
- racism
- religion
- role
- socialisation
- stratification
- structural theory
- structure of society
- superstructure
- underclass
- upper class
- value
- working class

Key Studies

- Ballard
- Bourdieu
- Coates and Silburn
- Durkheim
- Gershuny
- Gillespie
- Hall
- Modood et al.
- Oakley
- Schudson
- Sugarman

The Individual and Society

You may think you know all the definitions, but it's a good idea to check. The best way to do that is to try these questions. You can check your answers by looking up the words in **bold**. *(These questions are for OCR, but are also useful for AQA.)*

Questions

1. Define the following terms:
   - a) **norm**
   - b) **value**
   - c) **identity**
   - d) **role**

2. Outline the main principles of the following branches of sociology:
   - a) **Functionalism**
   - b) **Marxism**
   - c) **Interactionism**

3. What is **labelling theory**?

4. Define each of the following:
   - a) **upper class**
   - b) **middle class**
   - c) **working class**
   - d) **underclass**

5. Who said that the upper class uses **cultural capital** to stay at the top of society?

6. Describe what is meant by the **infrastructure** and the **superstructure** of society.

7. How do **primary** and **secondary socialisation** occur?

8. Describe the four types of gender socialisation identified by **Oakley**.

9. What is the main difference between **structural** and **action** theories?

10. Give two examples each of **ascribed status** and **achieved status**.

11. How many classes does the **NS-SEC** divide people into?

12. Describe **Ballard**'s findings with regard to ethnic identity.

13. Explain what is meant by **deviance**. What is the opposite of deviance?

14. Give two examples of the situational constraints that **Coates and Silburn** identified as factors preventing people from breaking out of poverty.

15. What did **Sugarman** suggest as a reason for the different behaviour of working class and middle class children?

Families and Households

Check you're comfortable with all the terms and sociologists listed below. If there are any that you haven't seen before, look them up and learn the definition. *(This topic is for both AQA and OCR.)*

Key Terms

• childhood

• conjugal roles

• extended family

• family structure

• gender

• household

• husband controlled pooling

• kinship

• nuclear family

• patriarchy

• primary socialisation

• symmetrical family

Key Studies

• Ansley

• Aries

• Bott

• Boulton

• British Attitudes Survey

• Delphy and Leonard

• Edgell

• Engels

• Ferri and Smith

• Laslett

• Modood et al.

• Morgan

• Murdock

• Murray

• Oakley

• Pahl

• Parsons

• Phillips

• Stacey

• Willmott and Young

• Zaretsky

Extended Concepts and Theories

• culture of dependency

• feminism

• Functionalism

• industrialisation

• Marxism

• New Right

• Postmodernism

• social construct

• social policy

• status

Families and Households

Have a look at the questions below. If you can answer them all, you should be confident writing about the topic of **families and households**. *(The questions are for both AQA and OCR.)*

Questions

1.   Define the terms **nuclear family** and **extended family**.

2.   What was the impact of industrialisation on **family structure**?

3.   What did **Murdock** say were the four basic functions of the nuclear family?

4.   What were **Morgan**'s main criticisms of Murdock's view of the family?

5.   What were the views of the following sociologists regarding the function of the family?
     a)   **Engels**
     b)   **Zaretsky**

6.   For each of these sociologists, say what branch of sociology they're from, and outline their main views on the family:
     a)   **Delphy and Leonard**
     b)   **Stacey**

7.   Describe the three stages of British family structure described by **Willmott and Young**.

8.   Define the term **conjugal roles**.

9.   Describe the findings of the following sociologists regarding conjugal roles:
     a)   **Bott**
     b)   **Edgell**

10. a)   Which sociologist found that the most common form of family financial management was "**husband controlled pooling**"?
     b)   What does this term mean?

11. What do **New Right** sociologists believe is the best type of family for society?

12. What did **Aries** mean when he said there was a "cult of the child"?

13. Briefly describe the findings of the **British Attitudes Survey** (1991).

Health

The terms and concepts on this page are all related to **health**. If you have trouble with any of them, look back at the definitions section and learn the definition. *(This topic is for AQA only.)*

Key Terms

- biomedical model of health
- care in the community
- cultural deprivation theory
- iatrogenesis
- institutionalisation
- inverse care law
- medical elite
- medicalisation of childbirth
- mental illness
- mortification of the self
- National Health Service (NHS)
- social model of health

Key Studies

- Busfield
- Cartwright and O'Brien
- Doyal and Pennell
- Goffman
- Gough
- Hart
- Howlett and Ashley
- Illich
- Laing
- Le Grand
- McKeown
- Navarro
- Nicolson
- Szasz
- Tudor Hart
- Weber

Extended Concepts and Theories

- class
- feminism
- Functionalism
- Marxism
- social construct
- working class

Health

There aren't a huge number of definitions to learn for **health**. Have a look through the list on the other page, then try these questions to make sure you really know them all. *(For AQA only.)*

Questions

1. What is the main belief behind the **biomedical model of health**?

2. List the five features of the biomedical model identified by **Hart**.

3. a) Which sociologist described different kinds of **iatrogenesis**?
    b) List and briefly describe the 3 different kinds of **iatrogenesis**.

4. How does the **social model of health** differ from the biomedical model?

5. Which model of health did **McKeown** believe in?

6. What were **Howlett and Ashley**'s findings, regarding a link between class and health?

7. a) Define the term "**mortification of the self**".
    b) Which sociologist coined this phrase?

8. Describe the attitudes of the following sociologists towards mental health:
    a) **Busfield**
    b) **Laing**
    c) **Szasz**

9. What is meant by the term **institutionalisation**?

10. a) Describe the **inverse care law**.
    b) Who first came up with this theory?

11. How did **Gough**'s and **Navarro**'s opinions on the NHS differ?

12. What factor did **Cartwright and O'Brien** believe had an impact on the way that doctors and patients interact?

13. What does the term **medical elite** mean?

14. Say **Szasz** without sounding drunk.

The Mass Media

The **mass media** is a big topic in sociology. It looks like a lot, but if you know all the terms listed below, you're well on the way to getting your head round it. *(This topic is for both AQA and OCR.)*

Key Terms

- agenda-setting
- bias
- censorship
- cross media ownership
- cultural effects theory
- gate-keeping
- hegemony
- hyperreality
- hypodermic syringe theory
- intertextual response
- libel laws
- mass media
- media messages
- media text
- message trajectory
- moral panic
- news values
- opinion leader
- Postmodernism
- preferred reading
- Press Complaints Commission
- selective filter model
- structured interpretation model
- two-step flow model
- uses and gratifications theory

Key Studies

- Bagdikian
- Bandura, Ross and Ross
- Baudrillard
- Biggs
- Blumler and Katz
- Cohen, Stan
- Croteau and Hoynes
- Cumberbatch
- Cumberbatch and Negrine
- Featherstone and Hepworth
- Ferguson
- Gans
- Glasgow University Media Group
- Glennon and Butsch
- Gray
- Greenberg et al.
- Hall
- Hartmann and Husband
- Hermes
- Hobson
- Jones
- Katz and Lazarsfeld
- Lull
- McQuail
- McRobbie
- Marcuse
- Miliband
- Morley
- Orbach
- Rutherford
- Signorelli
- Tuchman
- Turkle
- Van Dijk
- Wolf

Extended Concepts and Theories

- Marxism
- norm
- Pluralism
- stereotype

The Mass Media

Have a look at the questions below on the **mass media**. If there are any you're not sure about, look up the word in bold in the main dictionary section and learn it. *(This topic is for both AQA and OCR.)*

Questions

1. Give an example of **cross media ownership**.

2. How is the idea of **hegemony** important to neo-Marxist views about the mass media?

3. Describe the four stages that **media messages** go through.

4. What did **Katz and Lazarsfeld** believe about the media's influence on an audience's opinions?

5. Describe the theory behind the **two-step flow model**.

6. What were **Glennon and Butsch**'s conclusions about class stereotypes in the media?

7. a) Who first used the term **moral panic**?
   b) Describe what happens in a **moral panic**.

8. Describe the **hypodermic syringe theory**.

9. Describe what is meant by each of the following terms:
   a) **intertextual response**   b) **message trajectory**

10. Describe each of the following theories of audience interpretation, and name a study supporting each one:
    a) **uses and gratifications theory**   b) **selective filter model**
    c) **structured interpretation model**

11. What did **Ferguson**, **McRobbie** and **Tuchman** say regarding media messages about women?

12. Give an example of a **Postmodern** theory about the media.

13. Describe the following journalistic practices:
    a) **agenda-setting**   b) **gate-keeping**

14. Name the sociologist who introduced the concept of **hyperreality**.

Education

"We don't need no education." So sang Pink Floyd. But there are some who disagree with this stance. Here's a list of people and terms that relate to **education**. *(This topic is for AQA only.)*

Key Terms

- Butler Act
- comprehensive schools
- hidden curriculum
- Ofsted
- principles of stratification
- tripartite system
- vocational education

Key Studies

- Althusser
- Becker
- Bernstein
- Bourdieu
- Bowles and Gintis
- Davis and Moore
- Douglas
- Driver and Ballard
- Durkheim
- Eysenck
- Fuller
- Gillborn
- Halsey
- Hyman
- Illich
- Keddie
- Kelly
- Labov
- Mac an Ghaill
- Mirza
- Mitsos and Browne
- Modood et al.
- Parsons
- Sharpe
- Spender
- Stanworth
- Sugarman
- Swann Report
- Willis
- Wright

Extended Concepts and Theories

- class
- consensus
- cultural deprivation theory
- deferred gratification
- ethnicity
- Functionalism
- gender
- immediate gratification
- labelling theory
- material deprivation
- norm
- self-fulfilling prophecy
- subculture
- third way politics
- value

Education

You know the drill by now. Try and answer the questions below on **education**. If you struggle with any of them, look up the word in bold and learn the definition. *(These questions are just for AQA.)*

Questions

1. What did **Althusser** believe was the function of education?

2. a) What is meant by the term **hidden curriculum**?
   b) Why did **Bowles and Gintis** believe the hidden curriculum was important?

3. What were **Illich**'s views regarding education?

4. Explain **labelling theory** and the "**self-fulfilling prophecy** of educational failure".

5. What did **Bourdieu** believe was the reason that upper and middle class children have more success at school than working class children?

6. a) Name two sociologists who thought that **material deprivation** was a big factor affecting levels of educational achievement.
   b) Describe the conclusions of each of the sociologists that you named in a).

7. How does **cultural deprivation theory** explain differential educational achievement?

8. Explain the terms **immediate gratification** and **deferred gratification**, and how they could be said to be important in explaining achievement at school.

9. For each of the following sociologists, describe their findings on the relationship between ethnicity and educational achievement:
   a) **Fuller**
   b) **Gillborn**
   c) **Mirza**

10. Explain the theories of **Sharpe** and **Mitsos and Browne**, regarding why girls now do better at school than boys.

11. Describe the school system that was introduced by the **Butler Act**.

12. Briefly describe the findings of the **Swann Report**.

13. What reason did **Willis** suggest for the formation of anti-school subcultures by working class boys?

Wealth, Poverty and Welfare

You need to know both sides of the arguments about **wealth, poverty and welfare**, before you go writing strongly worded letters to the newspaper or ringing Jeremy Vine. *(This topic is for AQA only*

Key Terms

- benefits
- class
- culture of dependency
- design for life
- market situation
- marketable wealth
- National Health Service
- New Welfare Contract
- non-marketable wealth
- poverty
- situational constraints theory
- social democratic theory
- underclass
- unemployment
- wealth
- Welfare State

Key Studies

- Beveridge Report
- Davis and Moore
- Dean and Taylor-Gooby
- Kincaid
- Le Grand
- Lewis
- Mack and Lansley
- Marsland
- Murray
- Piachaud
- Rowntree
- Spencer
- Townsend
- Walker and Walker
- Westergaard and Resler

Extended Concepts and Theories

- capitalism
- ethnicity
- Functionalism
- Marxism
- New Right
- social policy
- Social Trends
- third way politics
- Weber

Wealth, Poverty and Welfare

Now that you've looked over that list of definitions covering **wealth, poverty and welfare**, it's time to see whether you **really** know them or not. It's not that I don't trust you... honest. *(For AQA only.)*

Questions

1. Define the following terms:
    a) **marketable wealth**   b) **non-marketable wealth**

2. Name the "five great evils" of society that the **Beveridge Report** aimed to wipe out.

3. Explain the difference between **absolute poverty** and **relative poverty**.

4. a) What methods did **Townsend** use to measure poverty?
    b) What was **Townsend**'s view on poverty?

5. What did Lewis mean by a **design for life**?

6. a) How does **situational constraints theory** differ from Lewis's theory about poverty?
    b) Describe a study that supports **situational constraints theory**.

7. What views about poverty did the following sociologists hold?
    a) **Kincaid**
    b) **Dean and Taylor-Gooby**
    c) **Spencer**
    d) **Westergaard and Resler**

8. How do **social democrats** believe poverty should be tackled?

9. Name and describe the four sectors of **welfare provision** in the UK.

10. Define and give an example of each of the following terms:
    a) selective **benefits**
    b) universal **benefits**

11. What does **Murray** believe about the effects of welfare benefits?

12. Describe the views of one other **New Right** sociologist regarding benefits.

13. What did Weber mean when he referred to a person's **market situation**?

14. Briefly describe three different types of **unemployment**.

Work and Leisure

Check you know all these terms and the sociologists who came up with them. If you do then you shouldn't have much trouble with exam questions on **work and leisure**. *(This topic is for AQA only*

Key Terms

- absenteeism
- affluent workers
- agitator
- alienation of labour
- automation
- capitalism
- critical junctures
- deskilling
- false needs
- flexible worker
- Fordism
- happy robots
- industrial action
- industrialisation
- industrialism
- leisure
- life space
- peripheral worker
- scientific management

- social determinism
- strike
- technological determinism
- trade union
- unemployment
- work to rule

Key Studies

- Atkinson
- Blauner
- Braverman
- Edwards and Scullion
- Friedmann
- Goldthorpe et al.
- Grint
- Grint and Woolgar
- Kerr and Siegel
- Keynes
- Lane and Roberts
- Lash and Urry

- Marcuse
- Parker
- Pollert
- Scraton
- Thompson
- Wright Mills
- Zimbalist
- Zuboff

Extended Concepts and Theories

- anomie
- feminism
- globalisation
- Marxism

Work and Leisure

Just for a change, I'm going to tell you not to bother with these questions on **work and leisure**. No, just kidding, get them done immediately. You'll thank me in the end. *(This topic is for AQA only.)*

Questions

1. How does **Fordism** work? What system of management was it based on?

2. What were the findings of the **Braverman** thesis?

3. a) In what ways is post-**Fordism** different from Fordism?
   b) What did **Atkinson** find regarding how post-Fordist companies organise their workforce?

4. a) How does the idea of neo-**Fordism** differ from post-Fordism?
   b) Describe the findings of two sociologists who see modern production as neo-Fordist.

5. What is meant by **alienation of labour**?

6. Describe the findings of **Blauner** and **Goldthorpe et al.** regarding alienation.

7. What did **Marcuse** mean by the terms "false needs" and "happy robots"?

8. Name four types of **industrial action**.

9. What did the following sociologists conclude about why strikes start?
   a) **Kerr and Siegel**   b) **Lane and Roberts**
   c) **Edwards and Scullion**

10. Explain the main difference between **technological determinism** and **social determinism**.

11. Outline the views of the following sociologists regarding technology in the workplace.
    a) **Friedmann**   b) **Zimbalist**   c) **Zuboff**

12. What is meant by the following terms?
    a) cyclical **unemployment**
    b) frictional **unemployment**
    c) structural **unemployment**

13. List the five types of **life space** identified by Parker.

Religion

A lot of those sociologists (the feminists in particular) aren't too keen on religion, but I'll say this for it — the list of definitions you have to learn is pleasantly short. *(This topic is for OCR only.)*

Key Terms

- Calvinism
- church
- civil religion
- cult
- denomination
- desacrilisation
- differentiation
- disengagement
- ecclesia
- fundamentalism
- millenarianism
- New Age Movement
- New Religious Movement (NRM)
- Rastafarianism
- religion
- religious pluralism
- sect
- secularisation
- spiritual shopper

Key Studies

- Bruce
- Daly
- Halevy
- Heelas
- Herberg
- Maduro
- Malinowski
- Melton
- Troeltsch
- Wallis
- Weber
- Wilson

Extended Concepts and Theories

- false consciousness
- Functionalism
- fundamentalism
- ideology
- Marxism
- New Right
- patriarchy

Religion

Opium of the people or the fabric of civilised society? If you can answer these questions, you should be able to give a convincing argument either way on the role of **religion** in society. *(For OCR only.)*

Questions

1. What four features of churches did **Troeltsch** identify?

2. Define the following terms:
   a) **cult**
   b) **denomination**
   c) **sect**
   d) **spiritual shopper**

3. Describe each of these three types of New Religious Movement recognised by **Wallis**, and give an example for each:
   a) world-accommodating movement
   b) world-affirming movement
   c) world-rejecting movement

4. What three themes in NRMs did **Bruce** describe?

5. What did **Melton** find regarding the growth of NRMs?

6. Explain what is meant by **differentiation** and **disengagement**.

7. How do **Marxist** views on religion differ from **Functionalist** theories?

8. What did **Daly** conclude following her studies of Christianity?

9. Give definitions for the following terms:
   a) **civil religion**
   b) **desacrilisation**
   c) **religious pluralism**
   d) **secularisation**

10. Compare the views of **Halevy** and **Maduro** regarding the effect of religion.

11. a) What does the term **New Age Movement** refer to?
    b) Give an example of a **New Age Movement**.

12. a) What does the term **ecclesia** mean?
    b) Which influential early sociologist first began to use the term **ecclesia**?

Youth and Subculture

All these terms are to do with **youth and subculture**. Get this lot clear and there'll be no need for yo to star in some future case study on deviance or self-fulfilling prophecies. *(This topic is for OCR.)*

Key Terms

• bedroom subculture

• conformity

• crime

• deviance

• juvenile delinquency

• moral panic

• neo-tribe

• rite of passage

• subculture

• symbolic creativity

Key Studies

• Bennett

• Campbell

• Cohen, Albert

• Cohen, Phil

• Cohen, Stan

• Colley

• Eisenstadt

• Gillespie

• Gilroy

• Hall

• Hargreaves

• Hebdige

• Heidensohn

• Hirschi

• Jefferson

• Kearney

• Lees

• Mac an Ghaill

• McRobbie and Garber

• Miller

• Mitsos and Browne

• Parsons

• Thrasher

• Willis

• Wright

Extended Concepts and Theories

• institutional racism

• Left Realism

• Postmodernism

• self-fulfilling prophecy

• working class

Youth and Subculture

I wonder what would happen if I wasn't here to tell you to do these questions? Perhaps the Universe would end. Better not risk it. Do the questions. *(This topic is for OCR only.)*

Questions

1. What is a **spectacular subculture**?

2. Describe the findings of the following sociologists, regarding subcultures:
   a) **Albert Cohen**
   b) **Jefferson**
   c) **Mac an Ghaill**
   d) **Willis**

3. Briefly describe what the term **bedroom subculture** means.

4. What is the main difference between a **neo-tribe** and a **subculture**, according to Bennett?

5. What was **Parsons**' opinion about why young people form subcultures?

6. Define the term **symbolic creativity**.

7. Define the term **conformity.**

8. What were **Hebdige**'s findings about Punk?

9. a) What approach do **Left Realists** take?
   b) Give an example of a **Left Realist** study and outline its findings.

10. What did **Hirschi** believe about crime?

11. What did the following sociologists say about female crime?
    a) **Campbell**
    b) **Heidensohn**
    c) **Kearney**
    d) **Lees**

12. How did **Gilroy** view black crime?

13. Why do youth subcultures form in modern society, according to **Eisenstadt**?

Sociological Research Methods

There are loads of **sociological research methods**, and you need to know all about them. This might seem pretty dull, but it's just got to be done I'm afraid. *(This topic is for AQA and OCR.)*

Key Terms

- British Sociological Association
- case study
- census
- closed question
- comparative method
- control group
- correlation
- credibility
- ethics
- ethnography
- field experiment
- Hawthorne effect
- hypothesis
- interview
- interview effect
- lab experiment
- longitudinal study
- natural experiment
- observation
- open-ended question
- pilot study
- primary data
- qualitative data
- quantitative data
- questionnaire
- reliability
- representative data
- sample
- secondary data
- social survey
- statistics
- triangulation
- validity
- variable
- verstehen

Key Studies

- Barker
- Scott
- Social Trends

Extended Concepts and Theories

- Interactionism
- Positivism
- Weber

Sociological Research Methods

Ahh, the end of the book. This is the last set of questions you'll have to do, so make the most of them. Make sure you check each one by looking it up too. *(These questions are for both AQA and OCR.)*

Questions

1. Explain the terms **qualitative data** and **quantitative data**.

2. a) How is **primary data** obtained?
    b) How is **secondary data** obtained?

3. What is meant by **validity**, **credibility** and **reliability**?

4. What kind of research do **Positivists** usually carry out?

5. Describe how each of the following types of **sample** are obtained:
    a) simple random sample
    b) stratified sample
    c) snowball sample
    d) quota sample

6. When is a **pilot study** carried out?

7. Explain the differences between a **field experiment**, a **lab experiment** and a **natural experiment**.

8. What is **triangulation**? Give an example.

9. What kind of questions are asked in:
    a) structured **interviews**?
    b) unstructured **interviews**?

10. List and define four different types of **observation**.

11. How are hard **statistics** different from soft **statistics**?

12. What did Weber mean by the word **verstehen**?

13. Briefly describe each of the following types of **observation** used in sociological research:
    a) covert observation
    b) non-participant observation
    c) overt observation
    d) participant observation